TEACHER COLLABORATION FOR PROFESSIONAL LEARNING

Facilitating Study, Research, and Inquiry Communities

CYNTHIA A. LASSONDE
SUSAN E. ISRAEL

Foreword by Janice F. Almasi

JOSSEY-BASS
A Wiley Imprint
www.josseybass.com

Library of Congress Cataloging-in-Publication Data
Teacher collaboration for professional learning: facilitating study, research, and inquiry communities / Cynthia Lassonde, Susan Israel, authors; foreword by Janice F. Almasi.
    p. cm.
  Includes bibliographical references and index.
  ISBN 978-0-470-46131-0 (pbk.)
  1. Teachers—In-service training—United States.   2. Teachers—Professional relationships—United States.   3. Professional learning communities—United States. I. Lassonde, Cynthia A. II. Israel, Susan E.
  LB1731.T37 2009
  370.71'55—dc22

                                                                                                 2009033971
Printed in the United States of America
FIRST EDITION
PB PRINTING

10   9   8   7   6   5   4   3   2   1

Contents

APPENDIXES

List of Figures, Tables, and Exhibits

FIGURES

TABLES

EXHIBITS

Foreword

I thought I fell in love with research when I began my graduate studies at the University of Maryland in the 1980s; however, the more I read and learned about research I realized I had always been a researcher from the minute I began teaching fourth graders at Kent Island Elementary School on the Eastern Shore of Maryland. If we take our practice seriously, and if we endeavor to create a rich learning environment that enables every child to be successful, at some point we realize that every teacher is a researcher. Each day in our classrooms as we work with children, we continually examine ourselves, our pedagogy, and the learners in our classroom. The data we take in consumes us as we reflect on ways to improve a lesson that didn't quite meet a particular child's needs, or the lesson that needs to be taught next, or a better way of reaching a child. As we reflect, we often raise questions. Sometimes our queries pertain to a particular student (What can I do to motivate a resistant reader?), a particular phenomenon (Why do so many of my students have difficulty revising their writing?), or a particular issue (What can I do to make my classroom more culturally responsive?). The ongoing reflexive process we engage in daily as we observe and gather data, reflect on it, make revisions, and take action in our classrooms is an invigorating process; but it can also be exhausting and isolating.

In *Teacher Collaboration for Professional Learning: Facilitating Study, Research, and Inquiry Communities*, Cynthia Lassonde and Susan Israel provide the tools with which to form, and participate in, collaborative learning communities that support the process of teacher inquiry so that it is not an isolating, individual process. They gathered these "tools" from a variety of authentic teacher research communities ranging from face-to-face district-level communities to online virtual communities. The collected voices are woven together to explain the process of how to build a research community and to provide examples of successful research communities. The voices Lassonde and Israel have assembled represent some of the best thinkers from university communities, school or district communities, and online communities who have had great success in building collaborative learning communities. The volume begins by providing clear explanations of the nature of collaborative teacher research and effective professional development. As well, sage advice is offered regarding tips for forming collaborative teacher research communities. From there, extensive information regarding characteristics of effective groups, theories of how groups develop over time, and ingredients for successful learning communities is provided. This information, coupled with the authentic experiences of successful communities provides a rich, descriptive framework on which to draw.

This volume offers not only a source of support for existing communities of practice, but also a model for emergent communities to aspire toward. The insights and suggestions offered throughout the text are sound, reasoned, and supportive. In my research on peer discussion of text, I have facilitated and participated in teacher research communities centered on how to create student-centered learning environments that promote critical thinking, higher levels of comprehension, and tolerance for diverse opinions. I wish this volume had existed during the initial teacher study groups in which I participated. Our groups often encountered some of the same difficulties about which the successful collaborative research communities in this text speak. I know we would have valued learning about how others organized their communities and reading about others' experiences and the manner in which they worked through their challenges. I look forward to drawing on the collective wisdom Lassonde and Israel have woven together in this volume in my future collaborations with teacher learning communities.

September 2009   Janice F. Almasi
Lexington, Kentucky   University of Kentucky

Preface

This book is the go-to source for educators seeking support for their research and learning and eager to understand how to successfully start and sustain a collaborative learning community. As evident in our research for our book on teacher research (Lassonde & Israel, 2008), a wealth of groups and organizations are beginning to support teacher research collaborations, partnerships, and study groups. If you are part of one of these groups or are interested in learning about how to form a community of learners, this book will help you and your group create an agenda, recruit and support members, develop as a productive group, and effectively work toward the goals that your group sets.

Through our work in teacher research, we have communicated with teacher researcher experts and practitioners from across the country. While sharing experiences and stories with these experts and researching the history and path of teacher research for our books, we noted that grassroots teacher research communities and support networks were springing up around the country and have been on the rise in the past several years. We learned about and explored online networks, university communities, district- and grade-level initiatives, and state-affiliate groups all working collaboratively—but isolated from each other—in their efforts to support teacher research.

We noted that educators appeared to be continually "reinventing the wheel" as they built their collaborations from scratch. As one teacher told us, "We completely made it up as we went along, developing our own process" (Adam Renner, Bellarmine University). This book offers ideas on how to set up such learning communities. It provides examples and advice from initiatives that are currently working to support teacher researchers and experts across grade levels and contexts that are leading and contributing to these groups.

ORGANIZATION OF THE BOOK

The book is divided into four parts plus an epilogue. Part introductions contain opening poems, connections to theory, and discussions to prompt readers to think about upcoming topics in the section.

Part One: Why Support Collaborative Research? introduces collaborative learning communities such as teacher research groups as a form of professional development by describing the rationale, connected literature, the power and possibilities of collaboration, and evidence of emerging support groups. This part describes what groups do, their benefits, and several model communities in which collaborative practices have lead to improvement in teaching and student learning. It will be helpful in providing background definitions and information for readers to use as rationale to gain support and advocate for their endeavors in initiating and supporting learning communities.

Part Two: Building a Professional Learning Community talks about organizing groups and conducting research projects. This part begins with the specific steps and protocols involved in conducting research and the stages of group development, and provides explicit strategies so readers can apply the information to their situations. We include voices from experts working in collaborative groups at various levels and for a range of reasons and objectives.

Part Three: Collaborating Effectively includes chapters on improving group dynamics by considering ethical issues and on leadership success strategies. We suggest guidelines for each and provide rich case examples and scenarios. We discuss challenges of participating in learning communities, along with potential conflicts and ethical dilemmas that might arise.

Part Four: Model Learning Communities in Action looks at school-based communities, school-university partnerships, and networking and online groups. The final chapter in this part describes a districtwide model learning community called the Fairfax County Public Schools Teacher Researcher Network written by our guest chapter author Gail V. Ritchie.

The final chapter, the Epilogue, highlights methods for encouraging longevity through professional reflection and collaborative ways of thinking to increase success. The Epilogue ends with final parting thoughts about how communities can find their pathway to success and how school leaders can support them.

At the end of the book you will find wonderful resources in the Appendixes. Valuable resources are listed, and reproducible forms are yours to copy and use with your study group or learning community in your school district. Also, there are questions to help you reflect upon each chapter and exercises to try if you are reading this book as part of an organized study group. These resources will help you promote, manage, and organize your collaboration. Feel free to adapt them to fit the context of your group.

HOW TO USE THIS BOOK

Think of each chapter as a unique resource. You do not have to read the chapters in the order they appear in the book. You might read the part openers first to determine their contents, then decide which parts best suit your needs. Begin with topics that are priorities for your situation. Another way you might use this book is to begin to collect resources from the list of resources in Appendix D right away. Gathering these resources as you begin your journey will ensure they are at your fingertips when members need them at critical points in their research.

A final suggestion for how to use this book is as a reference during the collaborative process. Read each chapter at strategic points in the process. For example, Chapter One can be used as rationale to administrators to gain their support for your group. Chapter Two can be shared to look at and gather ideas from successful models as your work begins. Chapter Three can be read to learn about the steps of the teacher research process. Then, Chapters Four, Five, and Seven can be studied when approval to proceed is imminent and you begin to form the group. Chapter Six can be used to troubleshoot problems as they arise. Chapters Eight through Ten can be used to determine what type of collaboration you want to pursue. Finally, the Epilogue can be read when your group is considering future directions.

ORGANIZING A STUDY GROUP

This book is ideal for use as a common reading for professional study groups interested in embarking upon collaborative teacher research learning projects. There is much to do before starting a teacher research project, especially if it is going to involve several researchers in collaboration. Being well organized with a plan for action will make the process efficient. Therefore, we recommend that the collaborative group spend time learning about teacher research and the collaboration process well in advance.

The group leaders might find it helpful to review the book carefully first so you know its contents and how it is set up. Then, decide how to proceed based on the personalities and knowledge base of the intended group. You know your group best. What do you think would help them understand the process?

Appendixes B and C provide suggestions for preparing before reading and responding to chapters after reading them. Even if you are not reading and discussing this book in a study group, the strategies listed in Appendix C will help you reflect on and think critically about your reading and the process of setting up and managing your collaboration.

THE TONE OF THE BOOK

Written in an informal yet insightful style, this book is readily accessible as a guide to scholars, classroom teachers, reading and special education specialists, literacy coaches, and curriculum coordinators. Administrators interested in promoting such learning communities in their schools may also learn from this book and pass it on to teachers in their districts to initiate relevant projects. Readers with varying levels of knowledge and experience with collaboration, teacher research, or research in general will find the book easy to follow yet full of practical information.

Special features are scattered throughout the book:

- *How to Use This Chapter:* Each chapter begins with a description of its purpose and use. This feature guides you through the process of setting up and managing an effective collaboration.
- *Thinking Together:* This feature includes recommendations on research connections, special tips, advice, or examples from educators in the fields of teacher research and collaboration. *Thinking Together* features show how concepts and theories presented in the chapters play out in real-life collaborations, and encourage readers to think about what they would do in a certain situation.
- *Collaboration at Work:* This feature shares recommendations about collaborations from experienced, practicing groups. You will read about successful endeavors as well as those that began less successfully. You will learn how groups and their leaders worked together to overcome challenges.

MOVING FORWARD

As you move forward in your work and in reading this book, we wish you success in finding answers to your questions through teacher research collaboration. We think you will find it the most engaging, meaningful, and long-lasting form of professional development in which you could ever participate. We certainly have.

Acknowledgments

First and foremost, we would like to thank Jossey-Bass Publishers, especially our editor, Christie Hakim, for recognizing the need for this book in the field of education and supporting the development of our manuscript. We also appreciate the time and hard work of Julia Parmer, Kate Bradford, Pamela Berkman, Donna Cohn, Elizabeth Forsaith, and Sharon Duffy. Also, Jossey-Bass's anonymous reviewers provided rich suggestions for improving our manuscript drafts.

We would also like to extend a warm thank-you to these folks:

Colleagues and friends who contributed their voices and stories to our book. Their contributions have truly made this book a collaborative effort.

Taffy Raphael, for helping us shape our survey.

The Mt. Markham Professional Development Panel: Lynne Byrnes, Casey Barduhn, Terri Stile, Julie Reader, Ruth Malowicki, Christine Maine, and Elaine Ruigrok.

All of the educators who responded to our survey, including Alan Amtzis, Gail Ritchie, Anita Long, Derin Atay, Cindy Ballenger, Bill Bigelow, Emily Van Zee, Paula Costello, Ann Dutton Ewbank, Carole Edelsky, Deb Eldridge, Fran Falk-Ross, Jacqueline Delong, Nancy Fichtman Dana, Becky Rogers, Todd Wanerman, Mary Linville, Linda May Fitzgerald, Rebecca K. Fox, Jane Hansen, K. E. Hones, Pegeen Jensen, Marilyn Johnston-Parsons, Barbara Kawulich, Andrea Levy, Robin Marion, Judith McBride, Daniel Meier, Kathleen A. Paciga, Diane W. Painter, Adam Renner, Leo C. Rigsby, Karen Blake Ruffner, Frances Rust, Jaci Webb-Dempsey, Neal Shambaugh, Sue Stephenitch, Ann Taylor, Debra Wellman, Jane Zeni, and Amika Kemmler Ernst.

The Authors

Cynthia A. Lassonde, PhD, is associate professor in the Elementary Education and Reading Department at the State University of New York College at Oneonta. Throughout her career as an educator she has valued and participated in teacher research and collaborations in various contexts. She is past chair and longtime member of the International Reading Association's Teacher as Researcher Subcommittee and initiated the New York State English Council's Standing Committee on Teacher Inquiry with Tim Fredrick. She also works with local schools to promote learning communities and literacy coaching.

Susan E. Israel, PhD, has worked in education and reading since 1989. During her elementary teaching days, she discovered how teaching reading comprehension strategies and higher-level thinking motivated readers and increased their self-efficacy about learning to read and write. She has worked with the Alliance for Catholic Education at the University of Notre Dame. She was awarded the 2005 Panhellenic Council Outstanding Professor Award at the University of Dayton.

Cynthia and Susan have collaborated on other books. They invite you to read these titles, which are strongly connected to teacher research and collaboration:

Israel, S. E., & Lassonde, C. A. (Eds.). (2008). *The ethical educator: Integrating ethics within the context of teaching and teacher research.* New York: Peter Lang.

Lassonde, C. A., & Israel, S. E. (Eds.). (2008). *Teachers taking action: A comprehensive guide to teacher research.* Newark, DE: International Reading Association.

The Contributors

Janice F. Almasi is a Carol Lee Robertson Endowed Professor of Literacy at the University of Kentucky. She has been actively involved as a teacher researcher and has collaborated with elementary classroom teachers for over fifteen years. Her collaborations have examined social, cognitive, and motivational aspects of peer discussions of text with children in grades K–4. She has also collaborated with classroom teachers to engage in book studies of classroom practice related to strategies instruction and peer discussion. As a result of her collaborations, she has coauthored the text *Teaching Literacy in Third Grade,* published by Guilford Press, with Keli Garas-York and Leigh-Ann Hildreth.

Leanne Avery is an assistant professor of science education in the Department of Elementary Education and Reading at the State University of New York (SUNY) College at Oneonta. Her research focuses on rural children's local science and engineering knowledge, place-based teacher professional development as a means of valuing and utilizing local rural knowledge in classroom practice, and the barriers rural children in poverty face in the era of No Child Left Behind. She was a public school science teacher for eleven years in a rural district in upstate New York, and she now uses this experience to inform her teacher professional development endeavors.

L. Kelly Escueta Ayers works as a fifth-grade teacher at Providence Elementary and has been employed with Fairfax County Public Schools since 1990. She is a project lead teacher–trained employee of Fairfax County Public Schools. She is currently a clinical faculty member with George Mason University's Graduate School of Education and works with professional development students. In 2006 Kelly was recognized by the Association of Teacher Educators–Virginia (ATE–VA) for outstanding research in a Virginia elementary school.

Lynne M. Burns has worked since 2006 as the P–12 literacy coach at Mt. Markham Central School in West Winfield, New York. Over the previous thirty-two years, she taught middle school as a reading teacher in grades 5–8, as a social studies teacher in grades 7–8, and as a self-contained teacher grades 5–6—always focused on helping students use reading and writing to deepen their thinking. Lynne's current special interests include coaching content-area teachers in strategies that support their students' reading comprehension and the use of storytelling as a literacy tool.

Carolyn Chryst is an assistant professor in the Department of Elementary Education and Reading at SUNY College at Oneonta in upstate New York. She has had a varied career path (actress and director, zoo curator, exhibit designer, college educator), which has lead her to focus on education reform efforts that improve teaching practices (kindergarten through college) and that support the learner's curiosity and innate love of learning. She has presented a workshop on "Infusing Theater Across the Curriculum" and coauthored a play for science discovery centers.

Lisa Corcoran moved to Albany, New York, in 1989 to begin her teaching career as a primary teacher in the South Colonie Central School District.

Michelle Crabill is a school-based technology specialist at Kings Park Elementary School in Springfield, Virginia. Prior to becoming a technology specialist, she taught third grade in Maryland and Virginia. She earned her bachelor's degree in elementary education from University of Maryland and her master's degree in instructional technology from George Mason University. She has participated in teacher research for seven years.

Lisa DeStaso-Jones has been a fourth-grade teacher in the South Colonie Central School District in Colonie, New York, for sixteen years. Her current professional interests include writing workshop and New York State history.

Cheryl Dozier, a former elementary classroom teacher, is an assistant professor in the Department of Reading at the University at Albany where she teaches literacy courses. She presents nationally and internationally on teacher preparation and has written two books, *Critical Literacy and Critical Teaching: Tools for Preparing Responsive Teachers* (Teachers College Press) with Peter Johnston and Rebecca Rogers and *Responsive Literacy Coaching* (Stenhouse). Cheryl collaborates with school districts as they redesign their literacy instruction.

Molly Fanning and **Brigid Schmidt** collaborate as teaching consultants for the Capital District Writing Project (a local site of the National Writing Project). Brigid and Molly were colleagues teaching English language arts for seven years at Farnsworth Middle School in Guilderland, New York, where Molly currently teaches seventh grade. At the time of the writing of this book, Brigid is taking time off from teaching to write.

Constance Feldt-Golden is an associate professor in education at SUNY College at Oneonta. She currently teaches graduate-level courses in mathematics education and action research.

Tim Fredrick is a doctoral candidate in English education at New York University Steinhardt School of Culture, Education, and Human Development and the cochair of New York State English Council's Standing Committee on Teacher Inquiry. Before starting his doctoral degree, he was a New York City high school English teacher and conducted teacher research studies on increasing boys' engagement in his class and increasing students' reflectiveness during their portfolio presentations.

Ginny Goatley is vice dean in the School of Education and an associate professor in the Department of Reading at the University at Albany. She currently teaches graduate courses on literacy instruction and theoretical foundations for current practice. She has worked with several groups of teachers in connection with her work on Goals 2000 and the Center for English Learning and Achievement. Currently, she is extending these collaborations to teachers applying for National Board Certification.

Susan R. Goldman is a distinguished professor of psychology and education at the University of Illinois at Chicago and codirector of the Learning Sciences Research Institute. For the past fifteen years she has been collaborating with educational practitioners to bridge research and practice. Dr. Goldman is widely published in discourse, psychology, and education journals and is presently associate editor for *Cognition & Instruction, Discourse Processes,* and *Journal of Educational Psychology.*

Jane Hansen has been a professor in the Curry School of Education at the University of Virginia since 2000, and previously she was a professor at the University of New Hampshire. For more than two decades, as a researcher, she has studied students of all ages, focusing on them as readers and writers, as self-evaluators, and currently as writers across the curriculum. Her most recent book, *Powerful Little Voices: Young Children Redefine Writing Across the Curriculum,* coauthored with five members of her research team (Holly Conti, Robyn Davis, Jenesse Evertson, Tena Freeman, and Dorothy Suskind), is published by Scholastic.

Pegeen Jensen has been a primary teacher in the South Colonie Central School District in Colonie, New York, for twenty years. Her current professional interests include writing workshop, current practices in Response to Intervention, and the influence of teacher language on children's lives.

Donna Killiany has taught in the South Colonie Central School District in Colonie, New York, for ten years. She is passionate about writer's workshops and teaching her students to be caring members of society and their classroom community.

Mary Ann Kramer is a program coordinator for adult literacy education in the city of St. Louis.

Susan Davis Lenski is a professor at Portland State University. Before becoming a professor, Susan taught school for twenty years. Susan currently teaches graduate courses in literacy, leadership, and teacher research. Susan has published more than sixty-five articles and fourteen books, including *Reading and Learning Strategies: Middle Grades Through High School, Reading Strategies for Spanish Speakers*, and *Reading Success for Struggling Adolescent Learners.*

Jennifer Lucius knows the value of actively engaging children. She's been a music teacher at Kings Park Elementary in Fairfax County, Virginia, for the past six years. During that time, she has worked heavily with integration of classroom content. Jennifer has created many curriculum-based songs and continues to share her music and passion for integration with colleagues across the county.

Christine Mallozzi is a PhD candidate in the reading education program at the University of Georgia. Her research interests and practices are influenced by her years as a fifth- and sixth-grade teacher. Christine has coauthored works on policy and adolescent literacy, reading curricula, policy-driven professional development, content-area literacy, and global reading practices.

Zanna D. McKay is an assistant professor in the Department of Elementary Education and Reading at the SUNY College at Oneonta, where she teaches Diversity in Education and History and Philosophy of Education. McKay has taught in Africa and recently completed a two-year sabbatical teaching in Vietnam. She has had articles published in the field's esteemed journals.

Barbara O'Donnell is an associate professor in the Department of Curriculum and Instruction at Southern Illinois University Edwardsville. She was a public school teacher at a variety of grade levels for thirteen years before teaching in higher education. Her current research includes teaching mathematics through the lens of problem solving and the use of dialogue in mathematical learning. She directs action research projects in the master's program and Illinois Math and Science Partnership (IMSP) Lesson Study Projects.

Taffy E. Raphael is on the Literacy, Language, and Culture faculty at the University of Illinois at Chicago. She directs Partnership READ, a school-university partnership funded by the Chicago Community Trust to improve literacy instruction through professional development, recognized by the American Association of Colleges for Teacher Education's 2006 Best Practices Award for Effective Partnerships. Dr. Raphael has published nine books and three edited volumes, and over one hundred articles and chapters. She has been a fellow of the National Council of Research in Language and Literacy since 1996 and member of the Reading Hall of Fame since 2002.

Gail V. Ritchie is in her third year as coleader of the Fairfax County Public Schools Teacher-Researcher Network. A national board–certified early childhood generalist, she recently returned to the school level as an instructional coach, after two years as a resource teacher for Fairfax County Public Schools' Department of Professional Learning and Training. Gail completed her doctorate with a dissertation study entitled "Teacher Research as a Habit of Mind."

Rebecca Rogers is a university professor and teacher educator. Before becoming a professor, Rebecca was a reading specialist in an elementary school and in an adult learning center.

Ilene Rutten is an assistant professor of literacy in the Department of Teacher Development at St. Cloud State University where she teaches undergraduate and graduate courses in literacy, children's literature, and teacher education. Her research interests include teacher education and grandparent-grandchild literacy connections. In collaboration with Cheryl Dozier, she recently published "Responsive Teaching Toward Responsive Teachers: Mediating Transfer Through Intentionality, Enactment, and Articulation" (*Journal of Literacy Research*).

Ann Taylor is an associate professor in the Department of Curriculum and Instruction at Southern Illinois University Edwardsville, where she is the director of the Elementary Education program. She has been a teacher researcher since her own public school teaching days in the United Kingdom. She is currently working with two second-grade public school teachers and teacher educator colleagues on the use of dialogue in mathematical learning. She is also studying how action research and lesson study support educators in researching their practice.

Melissa Wadsworth-Miller has been teaching English for the past fourteen years at Tonawanda Middle School in the city of Tonawanda, New York. She received the New York State English Council 2005 Educator of Excellence Award, as well as the Western New York Educational Service Council's Award for Excellence in Education. In 2007 she received the New York State English Council's Program of Excellence Award for a unit she created with colleagues that was based on teacher research.

Dawn Wheeler is the director of operations at Newmeadow Saratoga School in Malta, New York. She has been at the core of the school's development for the past twenty-six years and values the daily collaboration with other administrators and instructional staff to provide special education services to preschool children with disabilities. The success of the school's signature program, "Bridges," for children diagnosed with autism spectrum disorders, is testimony to the value of a team approach to education relying on the stability of experienced staff as well as the inspiration of young educators who join the team.

Jane Zeni has been in the English Education program at the University of Missouri–St. Louis for thirty years. She has been able to help teachers develop throughout their careers, from preservice through doctoral studies. As founding director of the Gateway Writing Project, Jane has collaborated and published with many teacher-led inquiry groups. She also worked to incorporate action research in her university courses to empower teachers.

We would like to dedicate this book to educators who have committed to trying teacher collaboration on for size. We hope it's a good fit!

TEACHER COLLABORATION FOR PROFESSIONAL LEARNING

PART 1

Why Support Collaborative Research?

INTRODUCTION

AN N^* OF ONE NO MORE
By C. F. Chryst
(in collaboration with Norm Parry)

From random thought, a burning question grew.
Gathered books around me searching reams of other people's work.
But still the question burned, a fire blown from place to place, igniting thought.
Deep conversations with paper people just wouldn't do.

I needed to know; I had to share.
Urgency built then bubbled out, bursting on friends and family.
Some nodded; some smiled; some derided.
Some cared as best they could with conversations, leaving both unsatisfied.
Silence crept into shared space.

---

* In research, N represents the number of values in a set of data. An "N of one" often refers to generalizations made on just one piece of information or information collected from only one person. Results reported from one piece of data may be considered less powerful than results coming from multiple data sources.

In a moment of bravery, the question leapt from my lips.
As I bounced my thoughts to a colleague, silence shattered;
Joy and excitement bubbled—a deep conversation ensued.
An invitation to her home to talk, to share, to think.
We explored a question that mattered to us both.

I, an *N* of one, once alone, gathered courage, strength, insight
With my now-friend peer. We, in a moment of bravery,
Invited another to join this quest to uncover.
New worlds of thinking evolved from deep conversation.
Surprised it did not feel like work, felt like breathing in fresh air.

Conversations in an airy kitchen around an oak table
Fed the burning question with ideas we, now three, cherished.
New questions rose, filling the silent spaces within this *N* of one,
Filling the spaces between each of us with energy.

No longer isolated in a sea of other people's words,
My voice is being heard. Another remarks, "Who wrote this? It's brilliant!"
None of us recognize the insight, but all of us hear the whisper
Of a new partner at the table—Our Voice—
Emerging clear and distinct, delivering forged insights from each of us
Born in fires of deep conversation fed by questions that matter.

The author of this poem is talking about forming a community of practice (Wenger, 1998) with her colleagues. This means that her colleagues and she become members in a group that is held together by their common pursuit of a shared learning experience. They develop practices—resources, frameworks, and perspectives—that help sustain their mutual engagement in the work or activity. Their community learns by "engaging in and contributing to the practices of their communities" (p. 7). By engaging in meaningful practices, they become involved in discussions and actions that make a difference to the communities they value.

The chapters in Part One provide insight into taking the first steps to open conversations that lead to improved student learning through collaborative learning communities that facilitate study, research, and inquiry and build teacher expertise. As you read these chapters, reflect on how the lines in "An *N* of One No More" connect to the approaches and research in these chapters. Also, the Reflection Questions and Study Group Exercises found in Appendixes B and C will help all readers focus on the main points of the chapters.

1

Improving Teacher Professional Learning

How to Use This Chapter

If you are reading this book, you are obviously interested in learning more about how to work collaboratively to support teacher research or how to set up collaborative study groups as a form of professional development in your school. You see its value; however, you may need further knowledge, information, and resources to substantiate its worth or to rally support from others. As a member of a group of classroom teachers, you may need to provide rationale and resources to administrators. As an administrator, you may hope to inform teachers and generate interest.

The purpose of this chapter is to provide background definitions and information for you to use as a rationale to gain support for your endeavor. When you are advocating for your project, you may want to provide specific examples, studies, and rationales from this chapter to inform others, such as administrators or funding organizations, of the value of teacher collaboration for professional learning. Consider creating a short presentation or a pamphlet that illustrates this approach for distribution to key people.

INTRODUCTION

One of the most frequent remarks we hear from teachers when we work with schools and organizations to set up collaborative learning communities, such as collaborative teacher research groups, is "We just don't have the time!" It is true that teachers are often overwhelmed with the day-to-day work of teaching and the many responsibilities that go along with it. How can teachers possibly fit even one more task into their days?

Collaborative learning communities can inspire and energize teachers to commit to this type of professional development—to become part of a community of practice—as a priority in their work.

Consequently, they begin to *make* time in their schedules to become members in these communities. They find the experience and the resultant learning valuable and the process intrinsically rewarding and enriching. Most important, they see how students' learning is affected.

We hope you will agree that one of our most important responsibilities as educators is to teach effectively. This involves staying updated on scientifically based research and teaching methods. We regularly attend conferences and workshops and take classes to develop as educators. As you will learn in this chapter, one of the most effective types of professional development is sustained, on-site learning such as that experienced through site-based collaborative communities. These communities can empower educators to seek out and prioritize professional development and can help members find and strengthen their voices as educators whose knowledge and experiences are valued. This newfound empowerment helps to perpetuate teachers' membership and commitment as it motivates them, focuses them, and encourages them to develop a voice.

We do have the ability and desire to improve student learning and to develop as professionals through collaboration. As the author of the poem that opens Part One describes, silence can be shattered when we are brave enough to share our questions with colleagues and have conversations that fill us with energy. We can and must make collaborative learning a priority in our professional development. Collaboration with interested colleagues can help us overcome those not-enough-time feelings. *WE* can do it!

WHAT IS TEACHER RESEARCH?

Teacher research is becoming a popular means for educators—classroom teachers, special education consultants, administrators, school media personnel, university faculty, and others—to improve classroom instruction and students' learning. Cochran-Smith and Lytle (1993) define teacher research as "systematic and intentional inquiry carried out by teachers" (p. 7). By methodically examining daily classroom practices, educators portray an insider's view of how learning happens.

What Is Collaborative Teacher Research?

When asked what stumbling blocks they encountered in their research, Mary Linville and Brittany Steele, teachers from the A. D. Henderson University School in Boca Raton, Florida, told us, "It's always difficult to find the time to implement an action research project and analyze the results with all of the other required teacher responsibilities." However, to overcome this common problem, they said, "We designed and implemented our project as a team, rather than individually. We kept each other on schedule by planning and working together throughout the project." Many teachers have responded similarly to these questions. Yes, teacher research is wonderful and needed; but who has the time? For many, the answer has become, "*WE* do."

Collaborative teacher research involves "individuals who enter with other teachers into a collaborative search for definition and satisfaction in their work lives as teachers and who regard research as part of larger efforts to transform teaching, learning, and schooling" (Cochran-Smith & Lytle, 1993, p. 298). Groups come together to support each other in a learning community, sometimes face-to-face, and sometimes online or through other communication methods, to inquire about compelling topics directly related to their classroom teaching and learning or schoolwide issues. These inquiries begin with a common question or concern educators have about issues such as how students learn, how to best teach students, or even issues that span multiple

 How does using the writers' workshop model consistently in grades one through four influence children's development as writers?
—Saddlewood Writing Inquiry Group, Pegeen Jensen, Lisa Corcoran, Donna Killiany, Lisa DeStaso-Jones, South Colonie Schools, New York

 How can we enhance the coordination between language and reading specialists to increase their effectiveness in helping such students in a classroom setting?
—Francine Falk-Ross, Northern Illinois University, DeKalb, Illinois

 How can a professional organization encourage and support teacher research so classroom teachers and their experiences can influence state education policy?
—Tim Fredrick, New York State English Council

FIGURE 1.1. *Examples of Real Questions That Have Inspired Collaborative Teacher Research*

grade levels or districts. Figure 1.1 lists several authentic questions that have prompted teacher research collaboration among colleagues. Note that questions here represent inquiries across grade levels, at a district level, and even at the state level.

Collaborative groups involved in teacher research are finding that the process provides professional development opportunities for them to reflect on their practices and to learn new knowledge (Mohr, Rogers, Sanford, Nocerino, MacLean, & Clawson, 2004). Teacher research involves reading and sharing ideas about current scientifically based research, classic theories, and effective ways to gather and analyze the information needed to answer the research inquiry. These types of professional readings and conversations help inform educators and, in turn, can lead to improved student learning.

In this chapter, to provide a foundation to frame collaborative teacher research, we first look at the relationship between teacher research and professional development. Then we share our experiences with teacher research collaborations, the rationale behind such groups, and what we have learned about other's experiences with these collaborative groups from our research.

Effective Professional Development

As educators, our expectations for students' learning have changed dramatically in the past few decades. We have raised our standards and vowed to leave no child behind (No Child Left

Behind Act of 2001, U.S. Department of Education). As a result, we have pursued effective ways to update and upgrade our teaching practices, knowledge, and skills. Many of us—teachers and administrators alike—have sought optimal professional development opportunities, such as conference attendance and in-service consultants or speakers, to teach us new approaches and scientifically based methods for achieving our goals for our teaching and, in turn, for our students' learning.

What Is Professional Development?

Simply defined, professional development is participation in opportunities that result in the acquisition of new knowledge, understandings, skills, or strategies that enhance and build upon our current knowledge. Our goals for professional development in education may include

- Advancing students' learning
- Exploring options and gaining new perspectives and ideas
- Learning new methods or approaches to advance our teaching
- Acquiring knowledge and skills that transfer to or apply to reformed curriculum
- Acquiring knowledge and skills that help us independently carry out new approaches by applying learned classroom practices

In addition, the U.S. Department of Education (USDOE), through the No Child Left Behind Act of 2001, mandates that all public school teachers participate in "effective" professional development that

- Improves teachers' knowledge
- May be part of a school- or districtwide improvement plan
- Helps students meet state learning and achievement standards
- Develops educators' classroom management skills
- Teaches how to interpret and use data and assessments to inform classroom practice

Furthermore, No Child Left Behind (NCLB) states that to be highly effective, professional development should have a lasting impact on instruction; be based on scientifically based research; be aligned with state standards and assessments; be "developed with extensive participation of teachers, principals, parents, and administrators of schools"; and be regularly evaluated for its effectiveness (USDOE, 2001, p. 1963).

What Works?

Disappointingly, we have come to find that many opportunities in professional development do not lead to long-term curriculum reform and do not meet the needs of the students in our communities (Henson, 2001). As a whole, research shows that professional development in the form of one-day workshops has very little effect on changes to the ways teachers teach, to the organization of schools and curriculum, and to what students learn (Gullickson, Lawrenz, & Keiser, 2000; McKenzie, 1991). The reasons for this are that potential effects are frequently weakened by lack of follow-up and inconsistencies in implementation.

The most effective programs tend to be in-service training programs that offer extended coaching with frequent feedback and follow-up. These programs tend to be much more effective than attendance at "one-shot," generic workshops or periodic in-service attendance in which outside experts who do not know the personal needs of your students, community, or district espouse their knowledge and discrete skills to improve individual practices (Dobbs, 2000; Gold & Powe, 2001). Research suggests long-term, site-based professional development opportunities engage teachers in the learning process, build from their current knowledge and practices, help them examine their beliefs with intent to transform practice, and allow them to explore authentic and personal questions as they develop answers.

There is considerable research to support that collaborative group learning is the most powerful kind of professional development (Arter, 2001; Garmston, 1999; Johnson & Johnson, 1999; Zeichner, 2003) and that collaborative teacher research is highly effective (Bullough & Gitlin, 2001; Cisar, 2005; Knight, Wiseman, & Cooner, 2000; Goatley et al., 1994). The opportunity to collaborate has been cited as the most important factor in instituting change. Stager (1995) suggests collaborative problem solving as the most effective form of professional development. Table 1.1 illustrates how the process of collaborative teacher research connects with the goals for professional development. You can see why collaborative teacher research is reputed as an effective means of professional development.

Collaborative teacher research is collaborative problem solving. Based on the literature previously cited, especially Zeichner (2003), and responses to our survey of collaborative teacher research groups, we propose that collaborative teacher research represents the epitome of effective professional development (Figure 1.2).

Many existing formats for professional development, then, are not effective and long lasting. So, how do we update and upgrade our teaching practices in meaningful ways that will help children learn and acquire skills as we seek ways to develop ourselves further as highly qualified educators? Based on our personal experiences and current research findings that examine various formats for professional development (described later in this chapter), collaborative teacher research fosters meaningful professional development for teachers.

TABLE 1.1. *The Process of Teacher Research Closely Aligns with the Goals of Professional Development*

Collaborative Teacher Research Involves:	Goals of Professional Development Include:
Ongoing conversations with colleagues	Extensive participation with colleagues
Developing purposes and potential research	Exploring options and gaining new perspectives and idea questions for a group study (or individual studies)
Researching the topic for a theoretical framework	Basing instruction on scientifically based research; adding to teacher knowledge
Collecting, organizing, and analyzing data	Learning how to interpret and use data and assessments to inform classroom practice
Determining the results of the study and applying them to classroom instruction	Having a lasting impact on instruction
Evaluating the collaboration	Evaluating the effectiveness of the endeavor

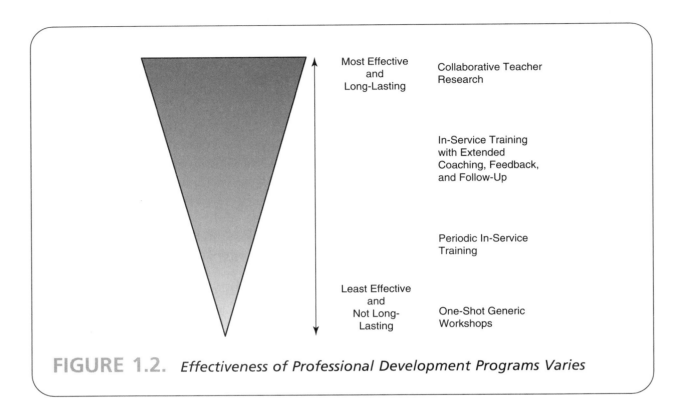

FIGURE 1.2. *Effectiveness of Professional Development Programs Varies*

COLLABORATION AT WORK: OUR EXPERIENCES

As veteran educators with over fifty years of combined experience, we have participated in collaborative communities throughout our teaching careers. For example, when Cynthia moved from being a fifth-grade language arts teacher to a college professor in an elementary education teacher education program, she had to adjust to the wide spans of ability level and learning styles between preadolescent ten-year-olds and preprofessional college students. She highly valued the benefits of teacher research in improving classroom teaching and students' learning, so she delved into teacher research techniques to reflect on her pedagogy. She also invited colleagues to work with her to add the more objective eyes of critical friends.

The first study looked at how her students, who were future elementary teachers, learned and comprehended texts through the use of the Book Club Plus approach (Raphael, Florio-Ruane, & George, 2001). A colleague, Karen, teaching a similar literacy course, had been using book clubs in her class, so the two decided to design a formal study. Having used Book Clubs Plus in her elementary classroom, Cynthia had been happy with learning outcomes and students' motivation to read and write about their books. But could this same method be successful with college students? And, to make it successful, what would she have to change from the way she used it with younger students? As the study progressed, the two colleagues asked a third to join the group. Overhearing Karen and Cynthia talk about book clubs, Krislynn added her knowledge of supportive literature and experience in teaching the same course Cynthia did in the past.

To make a long story short, after an academic year, the three concluded from their research that the students were receptive to the Book Club Plus experience (see Lassonde, Stearns, & Dengler, 2005). However, probably the most important result of the study was that the three had formed a collaborative group that had served as a tool to look intensively at each others' teaching and to discuss critically the effects of their teaching efforts on students' learning. They learned from each other through discussions of everyday events and observations in the classroom, sharing readings, and opening themselves to new ideas by listening to others' perspectives. In the process, they developed a supportive network that continues to benefit each member even today.

Throughout this book, you will read about similar learning communities. As you read, think about how effective this type of inquiry and reflection on practice will be for the teachers involved and their students. Also, consider how much more the groups of teachers will learn from their projects in a collaborative framework versus if they were working independently.

THE RATIONALE

Collaboration in teacher research has been credited with:

- Fostering reflectiveness (Schoenfeld, 1999)
- Triggering new perspectives in fellow collaborators (Morse, 1994)
- Increasing transferability of knowledge (Bullough & Pinnegar, 2001)
- Providing social support (Bullough & Pinnegar, 2001)

Louie, Drevdahl, Purdy, and Stackman (2003) report that "For over a decade, education faculty have used [teacher] research as an effective tool for both teaching improvement and knowledge discovery" (p. 151). In Cochran-Smith and Lytle's article (1999) about the teacher research movement, they identified trends that characterized the movement at that time. These trends included the prominence of teacher research as a form of professional development.

There are many arguments for collaborative teacher research. Probably the most compelling, however, is that it provides opportunities for professional development to be learner centered. In this case, the learner is the teacher researcher. Educators choose which questions they want to answer based on what is meaningful for them to know. When Cynthia's group studied book clubs, it was because the group members decided it was important to them to shape the method to meet the needs of college students' learning. They chose the question based on their personal quest to learn and improve instruction. They chose to work together because they had common questions and felt they could help each other by combining data analysis and interpretation insights, sharing current readings on the topic, and discussing how they would improve the method based on their combined results.

Frequently, a group of educators initiates a study because they experience dissonance or some uneasy feeling or uncertainty that is so gripping that they are willing to put forth the time and effort to find an answer through a systematic collection of information that will lead to the most likely answer. Ultimately, this answer is directly applicable to everyday teaching and improves instruction and learning.

According to Zeichner's study (2003) of collaborative teacher research that looked at five collaborative groups across the United States, the following attributes of such groups transform teaching and learning. Collaborative teacher research groups

1. Create a culture of inquiry in which teachers' knowledge and voices are invaluable to the research.
2. Invest in teachers' intellectual capital as teachers take charge of the research process.

3. Have a "multiplier effect" (p. 308) that helps teachers develop dispositions and skills by learning from each other's studies as well as their own. These skills extend to their working relationships beyond the research experience.

4. Create opportunities for intellectual stimulation and challenges that occur as a result of the group discussions.

5. Establish rituals and routines as part of belonging to the group. These rituals and routines help to build community within a safe and supportive environment.

In another study, Henson (2001) looked at how collaborative teacher research affected teachers' self-efficacy. She found that teachers did report they felt better about their ability to influence student learning more effectively as a result of their participation in the collaboration. What's amazing about this study, Henson reported, is that typically experienced teachers, like those in this study, tend to be resistant to changes in efficacy, or in how they feel about their personal and professional skills. However, this study showed that collaborative teacher research did make a difference in their self-confidence as teachers. Furthermore, teachers reported preferring collaborative teacher research to other forms of professional development because it allowed them to actively improve their instruction.

In our communications with collaborative groups, educators stated other reasons for coming together. For some it was a means to gain support in the endeavor for various purposes:

We wanted to support each other as social justice teachers and to do our work smarter and deeper.
—*Bill Bigelow, Rethinking Schools*

For me, it was a way to connect to others interested in research in Reading.
—*Debra Wellman, Rollins College*

We were teaching together. . . . Our motivations were complex and multipurposed:

- Colleagues needed publications.
- We were doing work we wanted to develop a deeper understanding of.
- We were already collecting lots of oral and written feedback from [our] students.
- We were using books and approaches that were new to us and we wanted to document what was happening.
- We adopted an adult development perspective that offered lots of possibilities for research.
—*Leo C. Rigsby, George Mason University*

For others, a common goal for large-scale reform drew a team together.

My science team . . . decided to change the style of testing to better meet our needs in assessing what our students have truly learned in the course . . . Since our school has all teachers become involved in action research, this was the perfect opportunity for us.
—*Sue Stephenitch, Highland Park High School*

We began looking at ways to develop a schoolwide inquiry curriculum at the high school level.
—*Judith McBride, McGill*

OUR SURVEY

In gathering material for this book, the authors were amazed by the number of collaborative communities that exist and are going strong across the world. The concept is growing in leaps and bounds. To gather information, we distributed a survey (see Appendix E) to various teacher groups and professional listservs, such as the International Reading Association (IRA) Teacher as Researcher Subcommittee, the Ethics Subcommittee, the Teaching as a Researching Profession Special Interest Group, the American Educational Research Association's (AERA) Action Research Special Interest Group, the International Teacher Research Network, and the National Reading Council. We asked members of these groups to complete the survey themselves and to pass the survey on to other groups they knew. We also did an extensive online search for collaborative groups and found a number of Web sites dedicated to supporting these learning communities. We approached these groups to complete our survey, too.

We found that respondents fell into five categories: K–12 educators, college instructors, school-college collaborations, organizations, and collaborations that resulted as part of college coursework. Although groups said they got together for various reasons, the one common thread was the work. They were all interested in the same goal: finding an answer or a solution to a question of inquiry that was personally engaging and rewarding for them.

This book is not only a resource for collaborative teacher researchers, but it is a model of collaboration and research itself. Throughout this book we will share stories and strategies from our experiences and from the numerous groups who responded to our survey. You will learn from what others have experienced and apply what you learn to forming your own group. We have also invited experts in the field to share their experiences and insights. To begin, see Jane Hansen's "Thinking Together" feature that follows. Jane shares tips and strategies for forming collaborative learning communities.

THINKING TOGETHER: COMMENTARY

Contributed by Jane Hansen

Currently, I am part of a collaborative learning community of university researchers and teacher researchers that has seven members: a pre-K teacher researcher, a third-grade teacher researcher, elementary math teacher researcher, doctoral student researcher in a first-grade classroom, doctoral student researcher in a fifth-grade classroom, doctoral student researcher in high-school American studies, and myself—a professor researcher in a second-grade classroom. We represent a range of experiences!

Our particular goal is to learn about students as Writers Across the Curriculum (WAC). To our meetings, we each bring two items for discussion: a piece of writing written by a student that week and a one-page piece of writing written by the researcher about the student's work. In this one-page piece, we write about why we chose to bring this student's sample. The writing we bring is diverse, and so are our analyses. Three of the many reasons for choosing an example are: it shows advancements by a particular student (one of our members is conducting a case study of one child), it shows the influence(s) of mentor texts (this is a particular focus of the pre-K teacher researcher), or it shows the influence of self-evaluation (a particular interest of mine).

(continued)

(continued)

At our meetings, each person reads the two pieces aloud; and we talk. We go around the circle, devoting about ten to fifteen minutes per person. Great energy evolves and carries through the next week!

Teachers' preparation before the meetings contributes greatly to the richness of our discussions. In my current group, we comment on what we learn about the students and about what appears to work (or not) within WAC instruction. We ask questions of each other to figure out what's going on, and we comment on each other's joys and concerns.

The third-grade teacher researcher I mentioned briefly learned from the pre-K teacher researcher that children who can't write their names can write. They apply markers to paper without qualm. Thus, her new student from Puerto Rico, who could not speak or understand English, could write on his first day in her classroom—and his classmates could respond supportively, including him in their classroom writing community.

The elementary math teacher researcher learned from interaction with me about student-generated rubrics, and her students created and used them to intentionally improve their written explanations about their solutions to math problems.

I learned from one of the first-grade teachers about the amazing ability of young children, in the fall semester, to create nonfiction texts—complete with tables of contents and indexes. Plus, for a particular child, this was his entry into writing. Nonfiction writing in science set the stage for him as a learner.

This anecdote describes my current learning community, but I have been engaged in similar groups for more than two decades and all have differed. Some met only to share their own writing, not their students' writing, or they shared writing they composed about their students. This experience gave them tremendous insider knowledge about what they did as writers—information they used as teachers.

THE BENEFITS

You have learned in this chapter that collaborative learning communities of research, study, and inquiry not only build teacher expertise and improve students' learning but also offer opportunities for communities of practice to form that create safe places for colleagues to explore, learn, and bond both professionally and personally. By now you must be anxious to read more about how research and inquiry can lead to educational improvement, which is the topic of Chapter Two. So, let's move on!

2

Initiating Educational Improvements

COLLABORATION AT WORK

The first model is written by two seventh-grade language arts teachers, Molly and Brigid. Starting off as colleagues who shared ideas, a close friendship developed. They extended their professional and personal relationships when they decided to try their hands at teacher research collaboration. They wanted to learn how assessment influenced their students' writing. This is a model of their collaborative teacher research project.

Model 1: Teacher Research Collaboration to Examine Students' Writing and Assessment

Contributed by Molly Fanning and Brigid Schmidt

As two seventh-grade language arts teachers working in the same building, we had for several years shared ideas about our common curriculum. Teaching and talking about the same grade level had helped us form a friendship that led to a natural collaboration. By the time we realized we were knee-deep in teacher research, we had already stormed, normed, and were performing very well together (Tuckman, 1965). In our professional relationship, we have grown from colleagues simply sharing ideas to intellectuals doing the work of research—asking questions, analyzing, and interpreting data.

The question that guided us was, "How can our assessment of student writing encourage not only a better final product but also nurture each student's writing process?" We had struggled with how to have our assessments give students credit for the work of getting to the final product, not simply be a grade on a piece of writing. We began to implement our version of achievement grading based on *Alternatives to Grading Student Writing* edited by Stephen Tchudi (1997).

Our new approach to writing asked students to include a piece of written reflection on their writing process along with their final product. Students also knew from the very beginning of every project the level of commitment necessary to achieve the grade they hoped to earn. Students became invested in their writing because they were allowed to negotiate how they would meet the criteria through student-teacher writing conferences and whole-class discussion; they gained control in an area where they usually had none.

We first felt the impact of our research in our teaching. We started to change and restructure the way we approached our units of writing and our writer's workshop classrooms. As we tried and worked through different forms of achievement grading, one of the most significant "aha" moments that we had concerned the importance of audience and purpose when it came to our students' writing. We had always taught these two concepts, but those lessons often came toward the end of a unit. Students were accountable for sending their writing to a real audience to achieve an A. As we talked and refined our work, we realized that although we knew that understanding audience and purpose were vital to successful writing, we had not made this clear to our students from the beginning. Our collaboration helped us to see the crucial context that audience and purpose had in our classrooms, and we moved these concepts to the forefront of our assessments and teaching. Foregrounding this idea changed the way we approached the structure of our writing workshops, the design of our lesson plans, and the way we talked to students about the framework for their writing.

Not surprisingly, this impact on our teaching spilled over to our students. We saw students who were more invested in their work. They appreciated having a clear concept of what they were working on and why. They also wrote in a relaxed atmosphere where how to earn their grade was not some big mystery they were working to discover. They had chosen their goal and were working toward it with confidence. With the pressure somewhat lifted, our students had an easier time finding their voices in their writing.

Like the recursive nature of writing, the success we were having in our teaching and with our students had a great effect on our professional lives as well. We began to seek out venues where we could share our research with other teachers. We began giving presentations at the local and national level. We also wrote about our experiences for *The English Journal*, the journal of the National Council of Teachers of English, and *The Record*, the journal of the New York State English Council. We look at ourselves not as colleagues who share their good ideas but as professionals who talk, ask questions, analyze, and interpret their work.

We encourage all teachers to reflect about their relationships with their colleagues. Take a close look at the friend teaching across the hall with whom you share your good ideas. Is it possible that person could be someone with whom you not only enjoy lunch chatter and teaching ideas but someone with whom you could unveil ways to improve instruction through collaborative teacher research? Reflect on the possibilities for collaboration that exist in your hall, your building, and even your district. How could extending these relationships through collaborative teacher research improve students' learning as did our professional collaboration?

POSITIVE OUTCOMES DEMONSTRATED BY THIS MODEL

- A personal and professional partnership emerged, strengthened by common inquiries and the pursuit of parallel goals. The underlying trusting relationship between Molly and Brigid fortified their collaboration.

- This type of culture of seeking new understandings through collaboration demonstrates proactive professional development for other colleagues. When colleagues notice that improved student learning, engagement, and commitment result from modeled communities of collaboration, they can become intrigued and eager to become part of the wave seemingly sweeping through the school.

- Students became invested in and committed to their writing. They were empowered and engaged as a result of the new approaches their teachers were incorporating into their instruction.

- The communication between the teachers clarified their understandings of what it took to get students to find their voices in writing. A trusting relationship and common goals allowed Molly and Brigid to step into new territories and try new ideas in order to improve students' writing.

- This research project opened opportunities for Molly and Brigid to develop their scholarship. They shared the results of their study through presentations and publications. The dissemination of their results will help other educators and students.

COLLABORATION AT WORK

Teachers in middle grades across two school districts came together to investigate how the use of students' interests in musical lyrics might improve their skill at understanding and interpreting poetry. Melissa and her colleagues worked together in this teacher research collaboration to find engaging approaches to improve students' learning.

Model 2: Cross-School Collaboration on Poetry
Contributed by Melissa Wadsworth-Miller

When I began my teacher research project, I had one goal in mind: I needed to convince my administrators and colleagues that there were more engaging and effective ways to improve student achievement on the state English language arts assessments than doing practice tests and similar assignments. Since the inception of these state standardized tests, it has been impressed upon many educators that the best way to prepare students for these assessments is to repeatedly drill with practice tests, the idea being that repetition will eventually lead to improvement. However, time and time again, I saw my seventh- and eighth-grade students struggle with these practice tests, especially when they involved analyzing poetry. They had tremendous difficulty uncovering the figurative meanings of poems. Moreover, they were frequently unable to identify the types of figurative language used within the poems, and they often did not connect with the subject matter.

Then, one day, as I watched a student enter school with iPod cords dangling from his ears, an idea came to me. Why not use the lyrics from popular music to teach the elements of poetry and poetic analysis? After all, songs are simply poems set to music. Implementing this concept would not only engage students who were auditory learners, but it would also motivate students by utilizing songs that they are familiar with and enjoy.

I believed this technique would be successful. However, I knew that before I could get approval from my administration, I needed supporting research to prove the validity of my hypothesis. I started researching the effects of using music in the classroom, especially for at-risk and special-needs students. After reading numerous journal articles and gathering the needed documentation, I presented my idea to my principal. He said he would support my attempt to implement this method on the condition that I get prior approval of all songs; furthermore, he would review the state assessment results at the end of the year to determine whether or not the initiative was successful.

Unfortunately, my colleagues were not as receptive. When the concept was presented to others within my department, many were unwilling to abandon their traditional test-preparation methods; others did not want to delve into the unfamiliar world of popular music. Instead of discarding my idea, I discussed it with two teachers from other districts with whom I had collaborated on prior occasions. Both were excited to test the concept in their classrooms and were anxious to start creating lyric-based lessons with me.

As we anticipated, student interest and class participation increased dramatically upon implementing these lessons. Students were able to identify the various types of figurative language found in the songs, as well as look beyond the literal meaning of the lyrics and comprehend the figurative meanings the songs convey. When reviewing data, we found test scores increased dramatically, particularly related to determining use of literary devices, drawing conclusions and making inferences, and recognizing how authors use language to create feelings.

Through teacher research, a simple idea that developed while observing students entering school turned into a program that benefited students in several rural, urban, and suburban school districts as others began to use this approach. The research also regenerated my teaching career in ways I did not think possible. Not only have I developed great friendships and working relationships with teachers from other districts, but I am also viewed in a different light by administrators and colleagues at my home school. After the research results became public, principals from my district asked me to sit down with members of my department to show them how to create similar lessons; several teachers have since implemented the program's techniques into their curricula. My school board recognized me with an award for the outstanding efforts I have made to improve the education of the students in the district. Finally, our program received the 2007 Program of Excellence Award from the New York State English Council. Teacher research has not only improved the education I can offer my students, but it has also given me newfound respect from administrators and colleagues across the state.

POSITIVE OUTCOMES DEMONSTRATED BY THIS MODEL

- As a teacher, Melissa was empowered by her collaborative efforts and the support of her administrators. From her belief that using practice tests was an ineffective approach to improving state-mandated test scores, Melissa ventured to find a new approach that would motivate students and support their learning. As a result, she changed her curriculum to benefit students' learning in meaningful ways.

- Melissa did not find colleagues within her building or school district who shared the same philosophy, but she didn't let that deter her. Valuing collaboration, she approached two colleagues from another school district to work with her. She did not give up or attempt to work independently; instead, she reached a bit further to find colleagues who were intrigued by her suggestions. In the end, by sharing the evidence-based results, she won over many district colleagues to her way of thinking.

- Hundreds of students benefited from this collaboration, as other teachers heard about the positive results of the program and introduced it into their curricula. Asked by her administrator to share her program with colleagues, Melissa has developed into a well-respected teacher leader in her school district and across the state.

- Melissa's group and school district were recognized by winning a state award for the program of excellence that resulted from this collaborative study.

COLLABORATION AT WORK

In this model, a music teacher and a third-grade teacher collaborate to inquire about the integration of music into third-grade content. They partnered up to investigate what resources were already available to them, to write original songs when other resources were not available, and to determine how to teach children to write their own content-knowledge songs. They valued the use of music as a method to help students remember and understand important processes and information. The following depicts how Michelle and Jen influenced learning and instruction through their collaborative inquiry.

Model 3: Teacher Study of Integrating Music in the Content Areas

Contributed by Michelle Crabill and Jen Lucius

We work at a K–3 school located in northern Virginia. The school's motto is "Together We Grow"; however, in the past, our specialists and classroom teachers taught their specific curriculum without knowledge of what anyone else was teaching. It didn't occur to them that by combining classroom content with the specialists' expertise, lessons would enhance and reinforce the curriculum in both areas.

Five years ago, Michelle (a third-grade teacher at the time) informed Jen (the music teacher) about an upcoming unit on ancient Egypt. Jen found a song pertaining to facts the students were learning, and taught them "Egypt Rap" from the "Did You Know" musical. It came as quite a surprise when Michelle's students returned to their classroom and performed their newly learned rap for her—memorized and with movements. The rap included many of the facts associated with the essential knowledge they were focusing on at the time. Students were excited to make a connection between what they were learning in the classroom and what they had been doing in music. This newfound and uncharted adventure paved the way for many other opportunities to integrate and reinforce the curriculum-required objectives.

The following year, we decided to pursue our collaboration further and study the effects of integrating music with core classroom material. Our collaboration focused on these goals:

- Using available resources to find songs that fit the county objectives for both the classroom curriculum and the music curriculum
- Writing original songs when we couldn't find necessary materials
- Teaching the students how to put facts into familiar songs or nursery rhymes

Concurrent with our study, the specialists at our school created a document called "The Monthly Planner," which became an important tool in promoting collaboration between the arts and classroom teachers. Each month, the team leader from each grade level would e-mail the team's planner. These planners were organized by the specialists in a way that provided them with weekly content topics of study for each grade level.

As the study began, many different resources were utilized to reinforce the content curriculum. The "Did You Know" musical and economics packet proved to be extremely helpful and provided many songs that tied directly to our curriculum and objectives. The students were excited to learn these songs in school and perform them for their families at home. However, we realized there were additional content areas that students were struggling with that needed attention. Jen could not find the necessary resources, so she decided to gather content information and write original songs. This was the beginning of the process of writing original songs that helped enforce more core content material.

Michelle's third-grade students were struggling with the idea of the writing process. Michelle had tried several different strategies (focus lessons, writing wheel, buddy writing, and so on). However, students were still turning in papers that did not reflect stages of the writing process such as prewriting, revising, and editing. Michelle was concerned. She e-mailed Jen with detailed information about the writing process in hopes that Jen could put together a song to clarify the students' confusions.

During music class, Jen decided to use the writing process with the students to create an original song about the writing process. She began the lesson by planning their writing. She wrote the major steps of the writing process on the whiteboard in columns, leaving room to jot down ideas about what each step contained. She wrote the chorus to the tune of "Muppets Tonight" and created the original music for the verses. After teaching the students how the song would sound without words, Jen and the students brainstormed to generate descriptors for each step in the process.

The class focused on each step of the writing process one at a time and brainstormed ideas for each line. Next, Jen taught the students an easy way to find rhyming words that would make sense in a song. They would write the first line of the verse, then focus on the last word. The students would name all the rhyming words to either the vowel sound or the ending of the word. This allowed them to help create the song in an organized way and reinforced word study skills they were learning in the classroom.

Once a draft was created, Michelle joined Jen and the students in music class to revisit and finalize their song. Michelle was able to confirm the content and assist in

(continued)

(*continued*)

rough moments to bring the song together. It was especially amazing to watch students who were normally quiet in classroom discussions openly participate. One student, who was very shy and quiet, added "who, what, where, and when" to the song when the class was having difficulty completing that line. It was an incredibly rewarding experience for both teachers.

After Jen modeled how to write songs with the students, Michelle encouraged the students to write songs, poems, or raps to review content during writing workshop. Once the students had become confident in writing these songs with Jen, they became more interested in writing songs on their own about things they had learned in class. The teamwork, dedication, and collaboration between Jen and Michelle made all of this possible for the students.

The impact of our collaboration has been exponential. It motivated other teachers in the school, and after sharing this research at the school district's Annual Teacher Research Conference, it began to have an impact on others in the county and in other states. After the second year of systematic collaboration with the classroom teacher and music teacher, 100 percent of Michelle's students passed the history portion of the Virginia state test for grade three.

Now that Michelle is in a different role as our technology specialist, we have found new ways to collaborate. As teammates, we are using technological resources (digital recordings and Smartboard use) to teach and record CDs of the songs Jen is still integrating. We have made it possible for others to benefit from their experience with collaboration and arts integration by making the songs available on the Kings Park Web site. This cross-curricular research has impacted the teachers at Kings Park and across the county. Educators from Virginia and other states have contacted Jen to get information about this outstanding teaching experience.

POSITIVE OUTCOMES DEMONSTRATED BY THIS MODEL

- The combined expertise of each teacher in this collaborative study allowed them to further each other's knowledge of content. While Jen learned about third-grade social studies content and how to teach writing, for example, Michelle learned how to help students write songs that included content knowledge.

- The students' learning benefited from this exchange of knowledge as evidenced by their participation in the song writing and the state history test scores.

- Michelle was given the opportunity to see her students' engagement in their participation in the songwriting. We can only wonder how her teaching might have been influenced by the time she spent observing her colleague's teaching, as it is not expanded upon here.

- Other educators can access the Kings Park Web site to find the content songs and use them with their students.

- The success of this inquiry has led Michelle and Jen to think about how they might collaborate in the future now that Michelle has a new position in the school as the technology specialist.

COLLABORATION AT WORK

This two-year collaborative teacher research study involved a school-university partnership. Concerned that targeted diverse groups were falling behind in elementary mathematics, educators wanted to look at how the integration of the arts—literature, music, and role play or movement—could provide background experiences with mathematics concepts.

Model 4: Study of the Arts in Mathematics

Contributed by L. Kelly Escueta Ayers

Sometimes the discoveries we make in teacher research surprise us, later causing change to occur in areas we did not initially consider. This was the case at one elementary school that embarked upon a two-year teacher research study. The data collected and analyzed led to a change for those closely involved, but also paved the way for change within the school for all students and teachers.

As educators, we often ask ourselves questions about how we can make change and affect our students. I have found that teacher research empowers me to examine my teaching practices; broaden my thinking; and positively affect students, staff, and community. It was during my school's second teacher research study, conducted in affiliation with a local university, that I saw clearly how my questioning could have an impact on many students. I had served not only as a classroom teacher and clinical faculty to professional development students, but also as the lead teacher researcher in our building through one teacher research study. Now, in the fall of the 2005–06 school year, I was to lead our elementary school in beginning its second teacher research study.

Our collaborative partnership used what we had learned from our first teacher research on "Mathematics and Differentiating for the Elementary Student" to develop the premise for our new teacher research. Consideration was given to the fact that although grouping students flexibly and using various manipulatives to meet student needs had a positive impact, many students who were in the targeted groups for No Child Left Behind (NCLB) were not achieving at the passing rate that we wished. After examining our data, we decided that background exposure to mathematical terms, concepts, and models was what our students in these groups lacked to be successful. Having a diverse population and being located in a city outside Washington, DC, continued to give us large numbers of these targeted students. Many of our students fell under two and sometimes three categories or more statistically for NCLB and the Virginia State Annual Yearly Progress (AYP). An example of this would be that not only was a student Hispanic, but he or she was targeted due to socioeconomic status and being a special education student. Our new teacher research question became, "To what extent does integrating the arts raise student achievement in mathematics?"

(continued)

(continued)

Teachers participating included a kindergarten teacher, a first-grade teacher, three fifth-grade teachers (including myself), and a math resource teacher. As a group, we decided to use literature, music, and role play or movement as our three strands of arts integration. During our discussions at teacher research meetings, we found that students at various grade levels in the targeted groups were still struggling with similar specific mathematical concepts, such as place value, fractions, and measurement. Students were exposed to literature, music, and role play during mathematics classes; the concepts were repeated throughout the year in various forms of the arts. This seemed to make these strand concepts concrete and understandable for the students.

At the beginning of the school year, my class was the lowest-achieving class out of the four fifth-grade classrooms for mathematics. My class was comprised of primarily Hispanic students and students who had not been successful in mathematics during their fourth-grade year. Many of my students had limited English language proficiency. I was fortunate to have the assistance of two English for Speakers of Other Languages (ESOL) teachers during the week. One teacher cotaught with me on Mondays, and the other cotaught with me Tuesdays through Fridays during the hour we did math. In addition, the partnership to host professional development students with the university allowed me to have a third person, my graduate intern, for half the year in my math class.

The low ratio of teacher to student, in my opinion, was crucial for this group of students. The impact of using the arts was also noteworthy. Results from our state standard mathematics examination showed a significant increase in student achievement for the Hispanic students whom I taught in the 2005–06 school year in comparison to the Hispanic students whom I had taught in the 2004–05 school year. When surveyed, the students clearly felt the quality of their instruction in math was better than previous years, too.

Though I was fortunate to have the assistance I did in my room, across the hall my team member, another participant in the teacher research study, did not have the same level of support in her room with her fifth-grade special education students. These students were pulled out for instruction to another room by the special education teacher and did not get the exposure to the literature integration in mathematics. When state testing scores returned for our grade level, the names of the students who did not pass the test created a "red flag for change" in the way scheduling and support should be given to the special education students. All the students who were pulled out during math instruction and were not exposed to the arts integration had failed the test. We cannot, of course, say this was the only reason for their test failure. Further study is needed.

As I reviewed our data, I realized what had really surfaced was an unintentional control group. This was significant for our research but even more important for the school as a whole. Administrators could clearly see that the isolation of these students may have contributed to their lack of success on the state test. Our administration was supportive of our continued endeavors as we began our second year of research and purchased literature books that integrated mathematics to give to every team in the building. More important, scheduling models were changed. No longer were teachers left without support for the special education students in the classroom, nor would students be removed for instruction. Coteaching became our schoolwide emphasis among all teachers, and resource teachers were coteaching in classes with ESOL students and special education students.

To me, the data we collect can make an impact on how an individual teacher researcher changes his or her own means of implementing instruction. Yet, when the findings and implications of teacher research extend to encompass the entire school and create everlasting change, it truly validates why school-based educators should conduct teacher research.

POSITIVE OUTCOMES DEMONSTRATED BY THIS MODEL

- At the beginning of this model, Kelly refers to this research as "a way for change within the school for all students and teachers." Later, she uses the phrase "everlasting change." Think about the power of those words and how they empower teacher researchers who collaborate and coteach. Teachers and teacher researchers collectively made a difference in the implementation of instruction and the learning of students not only for a school year but also, Kelly would say, over time. As a result of the successful collaboration among Kelly, her colleague, her graduate assistants, and her students, coteaching was emphasized by all teachers.

- This study also sparked concern for the scheduling and instruction of some students in the school who were identified as having special needs. Kelly describes a "red flag for change" in thinking about when students are pulled out for instruction.

- This collaborative study encouraged those involved to examine their teaching and broaden their ways of thinking. Doubtful at first about taking the time to integrate the arts and other approaches into students' learning, we may find that this integration is just what students need to succeed. Collaboration pushed those involved—educators from several grade levels—to think beyond their typical and perhaps traditional or safe ways of thinking to consider the ideas of knowledgeable others.

- The success and results of this group's first collaborative study led to a second study. This natural follow-up continuance is not uncommon. Learning together, feeling the support and excitement of the group, and seeing improvement in students' learning and development of one's instruction can be intrinsically rewarding and even contagious!

COLLABORATION AT WORK

Model 5 looks at a collaboration developed among university professors and graduate students, secondary science teachers from a local school district, and scientists. This inquiry group teaches many lessons about collaboration and educational improvement.

(continued)

(*continued*)

Model 5: A Science Inquiry Partnership
Contributed by Leanne Avery

Over the past decade, the science education community has been involved in creating university-school partnerships as a result of outreach mandates associated with grants such as those offered by the National Science Foundation (NSF). These grants require participants to set aside resources dedicated to science outreach in K–12 education. This outreach has resulted in the establishment of partnerships between scientists, university faculty, graduate and undergraduate students, and local school districts and teachers. In particular, NSF grants to kindergarten through twelfth grade require science graduate students or Fellows—students who receive the fellowships—to complete ten to fifteen hours per week partnering with local teachers in schools. They collaborate with teachers in teaching, bringing research into the schools, and developing curriculum. Research on the effectiveness of these programs offers us "lessons learned" about creating, sustaining, and growing collaborations or communities of practice.

One of the collaborations I was involved with was called the Cornell Science Inquiry Partnership (CSIP). This community brought together secondary science teachers, graduate students in the sciences, university science educators, and scientists. (See csip.cornell.edu.) Along with the NSF goals, CSIP had the goal of helping teachers gain familiarity and comfort in inquiry-based science teaching. One of the biggest issues we faced was teachers' reluctance to feel out of control of what is going on in their classroom (Uno, 1997, in Trautmann & MaKinster, 2005). Teachers who have not had scientific research experience tend to be fearful of leading their students in conducting research in their own classrooms (Avery, 2003; Cunningham, 2005). In addition, these same teachers also tend to rely on traditional teaching methods in which laboratory experiences are more "cookbook"—that is, the outcome is predetermined. A critical question for CSIP became "How do we provide professional development experiences that would help teachers overcome their fears of implementing inquiry in their classrooms?" We also simultaneously wanted to help the Fellows develop professionally as educators.

CSIP found several mechanisms that helped teachers overcome their fears of trying inquiry in their classrooms. These mechanisms enabled us to work with them in the context of their teaching in the era of No Child Left Behind. These mechanisms included partnerships between the Fellows and the teachers; several approaches to using inquiry; workshops for teachers, Fellows, and university partners; and a Web site with resources for teachers. We found it was highly important to create a supportive learning community with multiple opportunities for all members to interact and form lasting relationships. The support, reciprocal trust, and safe environment that were built through the partnerships, CSIP events, and community members enabled teachers to get beyond their fears of the unknown. Teachers were willing to take more risks in the classroom, gained confidence, and built long-lasting connections from which to draw upon in the future. The Fellows were provided with teaching guidance, strategies, and experiences from teachers and CSIP staff as well as feedback on their teaching and curriculum development. To implement inquiry and overcome fears and logistical issues, formalized structures such as professional development workshops, scaffolding between teachers and university faculty, and structured time for sharing in a safe and supportive environment are essential features that need to be in place to implement inquiry in the classroom environment.

The type of learning community created by the CSIP program appears to be a helpful model for other learning communities. The take-home message seems to be that in order to implement inquiry and overcome fears and logistical issues, formalized structures such as professional development workshops, scaffolding between teachers and university faculty, and structured time for sharing in a safe and supportive environment are essential features that need to be in place to implement inquiry in the classroom environment. Other research on science education collaboration also supports this approach (Avery, 2003; Avery & Carlsen, 2001).

POSITIVE OUTCOMES DEMONSTRATED BY THIS MODEL

- Collaboration provided the support and foundations of trust and safety that pushed teachers beyond their fears and uncertainties to try an unfamiliar approach in their classrooms. As a result, they were willing to take risks because their partners were there to guide and support them when things didn't work out. They gained confidence and felt they had a safety net below them upon which they could rely in the present as well as the future. Confidence and trust were strengthened to the degree that educators learned from the critical, knowledgeable feedback of others.

- Evidence showed that numerous structured workshops and events that encouraged the members of the group to spend time talking and sharing ideas helped them form strong, trusting bonds. These times to share fostered confidence and a willingness to try something new.

- By researching what others have written and studied, educators can find support to help us understand our work and build strong learning communities that advance the steadily increasing body of knowledge that exists in the field of education.

FINAL THOUGHTS

The stories presented in this chapter have shown how collaborations can link research to educational improvement of students' learning and teachers' instruction. We hope you have found ways to apply their lessons learned to your group's context and situation. We hope also that these real-life narratives have helped you confirm and evaluate what you are doing and have guided you to think about how you might make your work even more valuable in its connections and applications to your practice. In Chapter Three, "Understanding the Inquiry Process," we will learn how to better understand the research process and how to get colleagues intrigued about inquiry.

PART

2

Building a Professional Learning Community

INTRODUCTION

TREASURES
By Dawn Wheeler

I appreciate the stability of an old friendship.
It provides the surety of sameness,
The calm of familiarity.

I enjoy the exhilaration of a new relationship.
It offers the hope of discovery,
The risk of uncertainty.

I wonder, then, whom do I choose?
I depend on the calm and feel confident.
I challenge the risk and reach a new horizon.

Both have become the core of who I am.
I embrace the gifts both have to give.
I cherish my old friends;
I welcome the new.

Collaboration is all about working with colleagues. Though sometimes this can be rewarding and comforting, or provide familiarity and stability as the poem suggests, at other times it can be challenging. The author of this part introduction's poem suggests that being open to working with colleagues that we either don't know very well or have not worked with in this capacity before can provide opportunities to develop and extend new and existing relationships as we "welcome the new," discover things about others, and—through mutual interests, concerns, and passions—achieve goals and understandings at a level beyond what is possible when working independently.

The chapters in Part Two include support, based on recent and classic research and theories on the stages of group dynamics, for learning how to initiate and manage collaborative learning groups successfully. Part Two also includes voices from experts working in collaborative groups at various levels and for a range of reasons and objectives. As you read these chapters, reflect on how lines in "Treasures" connect to the approaches and research in these chapters. Also, the Reflection Questions and Study Group Exercises found in Appendixes B and C will help all readers focus on the main points of the chapters.

3

Understanding the Inquiry Process

How to Use This Chapter

Teacher research is a systematic method of inquiry that requires moving through a series of specific steps and protocols to scientifically investigate a classroom issue or practice. In this chapter we look at the steps of the process from identifying your research questions to sharing your findings with your colleagues to expand upon what educators know about learning and teaching. We also offer ideas for getting colleagues interested in inquiry. We offer a creative Readers' Theater script that you might use to accomplish these two goals in your context.

We don't propose that this chapter contains all of the information you need to know to become an established teacher researcher. Teacher research is very complex. It takes time, practice, and support to develop into a confident teacher researcher. One of the supports you will need is a comprehensive book that will guide you through the specific steps and protocols involved in conducting teacher research. We highly recommend *Teachers Taking Action: A Comprehensive Guide to Teacher Research* (Lassonde & Israel, 2008) because it breaks the research process down into manageable units. The book provides clear examples, defining concepts and using them in a way educators new to research can understand and apply.

The purpose of this chapter is to outline the teacher research process and to look at how collaboration fits within each step of the process. As you move through the rest of the book, keep in mind the structure and foundations of research that you learn about in this chapter. They will help to support your developing understandings about collaboration.

THE STEPS OF THE PROCESS

The steps of the teacher research process are as follows:

- Identify the inquiry
- Develop purposes and potential research questions for the study
- Research the topic for a theoretical framework
- Design and organize a research plan
- Collect, organize, and analyze data
- Determine the results of the study
- Share the conclusions and implications (Falk-Ross & Cuevas, 2008, p. 16)

To present and explain these steps in an engaging and contextualized way, a Readers' Theater script follows. The steps of the teacher research process are explained and embedded within the context of a discussion among several educators considering whether or not teacher research is right for them. This script, written by Cindy with suggestions from members of the New York State English Council's Standing Committee on Teacher Inquiry, was created to introduce collaborative teacher research to their executive board for the purpose of seeking their support. You are invited to revise the script as needed and use it to rally support in your own situation.

Possible uses for the script include:

- Presenting to a school or organizational board to rally support for a research initiative
- Presenting with a group of faculty to inform them of teacher research benefits and the overall process
- Presenting with graduate students beginning their first action research project

When the Standing Committee presented this theater script at the annual convention of the National Council of Teachers of English in 2007 in New York City, we printed out seven copies of it—one for each character and the narrator, highlighted one character's lines in each script, and approached participants in the audience as they settled in to the workshop. When people agreed to be actors and actresses in our play, we gave them their script and allowed them to look through the script for several minutes before the performance. When it was time to begin, we called the readers to the front of the room, lined them up side by side, and asked them to introduce themselves and where they were from. Then the narrator began to read. We were amazed by the enthusiasm and expression with which our readers performed. To our surprise, the narrator even provided mock organ music to give the flavor and drama of a soap opera. Sally, one of the characters who is often quite confused, made us laugh as we recognized in her bits of ourselves and our colleagues. Everyone in the room seemed to enjoy the format, and ensuing conversations indicated they made meaningful connections between the script and their own experiences with collaboration and teacher research.

The script can be an engaging way to begin the collaborative process. It gets people laughing and talking about real issues and concerns related to collaboration and teacher research. You may revise our script to fit your audience's needs or use it just the way it is. Enjoy!

TEACHER INQUIRY SCRIPT

Narrator: Welcome to Collaborative Teacher Research Theater. We hope you enjoy this episode of "The Guiding Teacher" starring:

_____ as Rock, a fifth-grade teacher with a question

_____ as Brook, a consultant reading teacher

_____ as Megan, the tormented and torn principal

_____ as Sally, the silly textbook teacher

_____ as John, an experienced teacher inquirer (researcher)

_____ as Hollie, an experienced teacher inquirer (researcher)

I will be your narrator as we enter the WoBeUs School and begin the next episode of "The Guiding Teacher." *(Imagine organ music here, please.)* In our last episode we heard Rock say . . .

Rock: Brook! Brook! Brook! Have you *any* idea how many fifth-grade students are creating meaning while they read? Do we know the effects of the comprehension strategies we are teaching them?

Megan: Our comprehension scores are questionable. What's going on in our classrooms?

Sally: *(quiet and confused)* What do you mean "What's going on?" I'm on page 23 today . . . tomorrow will be page 24, then 25, then 26 . . .

Narrator: In today's episode we pick up on a conversation between Rock and Brook. Sally continues to listen and learn.

Brook: We need to take a closer look at how we are teaching reading comprehension. What works, what doesn't? Then we can determine what strategies really help our students create meaning from what they read.

Sally: *(quiet and confused)* Create meaning? What's to create? The author does that.

Rock: *(hesitating as he shows confusion with Sally's comment)* . . . That would be great. Then we can tailor our instruction to meet the needs of the students efficiently and effectively. I'm not sure I know how to take a closer look, though.

Brook: Let's talk to John and Hollie. They did a teacher inquiry project last year. They wanted to know if their spelling instruction was effective. They implemented new instructional strategies based on the results of their inquiry. They're really happy with the results.

Sally: *(quiet and confused)* New instructional strategies? Did they get a new teacher's manual?

Rock: Well, I use the ELA Standards to support what I'm doing in my classroom. But what I need to know is if the strategies I am teaching are working for my students.

Narrator: Later that day Rock and Brook met with John and Hollie. Sally joined too, because by now she was as curious as she was confused. They learned a lot about teacher research, often called action research, or teacher inquiry. Here's what they learned.

Rock: What IS teacher inquiry?

John: Cochran-Smith and Lytle describe teacher research as systematic and intentional inquiry carried out by teachers. Generally, it begins with a question about a teaching practice that the teacher wants to examine and explore.

Hollie: For example, how can I motivate my resistant writers to really want to write? Is multiage grouping helpful to learning? Why do my female students seem to always choose the same series of books?

Brook: What are the benefits of teacher inquiry?

John: We routinely reflect on and talk about what we're doing in the classroom and how students are learning. But teacher inquiry methods provide ways for teachers to look at what's happening in their classrooms from several different angles by collecting information and then sitting down to analyze what's happening and why.

Hollie: In a time when teachers are being told what we *have* to teach, teacher inquiry provides evidence of what *we* know we *need* to teach. Teacher inquiry provides evidence to support what we're doing in the classroom.

John: When we share that evidence with other teachers, administrators, and policymakers, it empowers teachers by allowing their voices to be heard.

Brook: What is the teacher inquiry process?

Narrator: Typically, teacher inquiry follows these steps:

Hollie: First, shape a researchable question. Begin by making a list of questions you have about your classroom or your teaching or both. Try starting with "I wonder." This is a process in which you'll work toward framing a question that is answerable by collecting and interpreting information.

John: Next, do some background reading on related topics. For example, if your question is about writing pedagogy, you might read Graves or Atwell or Elbow and then see what current journals such as *Language Arts, The Reading Teacher*, or the *Journal of Adolescent and Adult Literacy* say about writing instruction. Continue to gather and read as you work on the project.

Sally: *(beginning to see the light)* Nancy Atwell! . . . I heard her speak at a great conference ten years ago. I always wanted to try her ideas but never saw them in my teacher's manual . . .

Hollie: Then, decide what types of information will help you answer your question. In a study on writing pedagogy, for example, you might want to collect students' writing samples. You might videotape writing conferences. And you might keep a teaching journal in which you reflect regularly about your observations.

John: Before you begin collecting this information or data, you'll need to acquire permission or consent from the students and their families. Ethically, you want everyone to know what you are doing and why. Then, later on, when you start to share your findings with colleagues, there are no questions about confidentiality or privacy issues.

Hollie: There are other things to consider, such as how long should you conduct your study and how many forms of data will you need for reliable results. The best thing to do is get a how-to type of book about teacher inquiry to follow or collaborate with someone who has practiced teacher inquiry successfully in the past.

John: As you collect your data, have a plan for how you will organize and analyze it. Organizing writing samples may involve photocopying students' reports, beginning a file for each student's samples, and a plan for careful identification of each writing assignment. The more organized you are, the easier it will be to work with the data later.

Hollie: A common method used for data analysis is coding, but there are many ways to go about searching for the answer to your research question as you read through your data. Coding involves identifying similar categories within the data and sorting them out. The data analysis stage of your project should be ongoing as you collect your data. But your final analysis will come at the end of your study when you really delve into what you have collected to interpret what it all means to you.

John: Here's where your background reading will help you. You will begin to recognize links between what you've read and what you're seeing in your data. You'll also probably find some discrepancies. These are what will make your study unique.

Hollie: The final step to teacher inquiry is when you apply what you've learned to your teaching. What implications does your learning have toward your teaching and your students' learning?

Sally: *(with conviction)* So, I don't have to follow the teacher's manual!

John: Many teachers have taken their findings beyond their classrooms to share with others. Conferences provide forums for teacher researchers to tell others about what they've learned so they, too, can benefit from the research.

Hollie: Also, many teachers are writing about their findings and sending them to professional journals. This venue promotes widespread application to classrooms *and* becomes a resource for policymakers listening for teachers' voices.

John: Teacher research or inquiry has been on the rise over the past few years. Administrators have begun to recognize it as a way to provide professional development for their faculty. Teachers are finding it rewarding to experience the professionalism of being researchers in their own classrooms and to share their work with colleagues.

Sally: I get it—inquiring minds want to know!

Narrator: Thank you for listening. *(Ends with organ music swelling in the background.)*

TEACHER RESEARCH TEMPLATE

In Cindy's work with Mt. Markham Central School's inquiry groups, they created an inquiry template to help guide the teachers' progress through the process. The purpose of the template was to provide the language for talking about the process collaboratively. The group emphasized that the template was to be used as a guiding worksheet, but not perceived as a binding contract among members. Members wanted to ensure that the process and the template could be flexible enough to meet the needs of the students and the collaborating teachers. See Exhibit 3.1.

Exhibit 3.1: Teacher Inquiry Template

The purpose of this template is to help guide your team as it proceeds through your inquiry. It provides an overall look at the process. Use it to spur conversations and to keep track of decisions. Toss it back and forth among teammates to keep everyone involved and on the same page. It is a *worksheet*, not a *contract*.

1. Briefly describe in one or two sentences what you want to study and why.

   _____

   _____

   _____

2. What questions about this topic do you want to answer? This will lead to your "researchable question."

   _____

   _____

   _____

3. At this point you might want to collect and read one or two similar studies about your topic to see what others are saying and how they have set up their studies. Look into the options for collecting these articles (example: online, ask for assistance from Lynne, the librarian, or your team).

   _____

   _____

   _____

   (continued)

---

4. What types of data will help you answer your questions? Select at least three.

_____

_____

_____

5. How long will you want to collect data to fully answer your questions?

_____

_____

_____

6. Before you begin, does family permission need to be obtained? (Permission must be obtained if student work or responses will be used or discussed in publications or presentations.)

_____

_____

_____

7. What instruments will be used? Will you construct a survey or a questionnaire? Will you use an instrument that is already published, such as a reading inventory or other assessment?

_____

_____

_____

8. Describe your procedures and time line.

_____

_____

_____

9. What methods will you use to look at and analyze your data?

_____

_____

_____

10. What does your data indicate? What are you learning from it?

_____

_____

_____

11. What do your results imply about teaching and learning?

_____

_____

_____

12. What have you learned about your own teaching in this process?

_____

_____

_____

13. How will you share your findings?

_____

_____

TEACHER RESEARCH TIMETABLE

Your group will design a timetable to guide your progress through the research process. The time frame, when carefully planned, will reflect the anticipated needs of the study and the expectations of your group. Studies vary widely; therefore, your timetable will be influenced by factors such as your research questions and how long you will collect data. You may also need to factor in school breaks so that you have ample time to read through and analyze data. Or you may intend to present your results at a particular conference, which will determine the length of time available to complete your work.

Exhibit 3.2 illustrates a sample timetable. Another sample timetable appears in Exhibit 10.1 in relation to the Fairfax County Public Schools. In the following section, however, you will read about collaboration among several teachers and grade levels. In their study, the timetable would look somewhat different from those shown in Exhibit 3.2 and later in Exhibit 10.1 because of the nature of their research questions.

Exhibit 3.2: Sample Timetable for Research Project

JUNE THROUGH AUGUST

Organize the group. Make short-term and long-term goals and plans. Plan the collaboration using information and forms from this book.

Read and discuss this book in a collaborative study group.

Read and discuss readings related to the teacher research process.

Form your research questions.

SEPTEMBER THROUGH DECEMBER

Develop your research plan, and begin an initial literature review.

Obtain necessary consents and permissions.

Begin and continue data collection depending on the needs of the study.*

Code, analyze, and interpret data as you collect it (at least weekly).

Continue to meet with the group regularly to discuss the process and the data.

JANUARY THROUGH FEBRUARY

Analyze and interpret the data as a whole.

Continue to meet with the group to discuss data analysis.

MARCH THROUGH MAY

Revisit the literature.

Determine findings and implications for teaching.

(continued)

Share findings with immediate colleagues (faculty meetings).

Determine how else you will disseminate your findings.

Draft writing and presentations.

June Through August

Revise drafts for possible publication. Submit to journal of choice.

Research conference options, and write conference proposals for presentations.

Determine next steps. Another research project for the upcoming school year?

*Length of time spent collecting data will be determined by research question(s) and design. Data collection may last as few as six weeks or as long as a whole school year depending on what questions you want to answer and how you plan to answer them (for example, what evidence you need to collect).

COLLABORATION AT WORK

Saddlewood Writing Inquiry Group

Contributed by Pegeen Jensen, Lisa Corcoran, Donna Killiany, and Lisa DeStaso-Jones

Four teachers—one from each grade level from first through fourth grade—got together to take part in a collaborative teacher research project. They wanted to study the effectiveness of the use of writer's workshop across grade levels by following a cohort of students for four years. Think about what type of timetable might be planned for a study of this dimension as you apply what you have learned about the steps of teacher research and the structure of research groups in this chapter. In longitudinal studies like this one, researchers should schedule in specific times to analyze and discuss the data regularly as it is collected, rather than waiting until the end of the final year to analyze the data for the first time. Researchers should continuously and regularly discuss and analyze data to inform the results of the study. These initial, ongoing interpretations of data are documented as preliminary results and may change as the study develops.

As teachers of third and fourth graders, we—Donna and Lisa—were often frustrated with the result of writing instruction that was inconsistent across grade levels. One afternoon while sitting together at a local writer's institute listening to author and professional developer Katie Wood Ray share the success of writing workshop across grade levels, we realized a collaborative study of the effects of this method could become a powerful, enriching experience for our students and for ourselves as professionals.

We decided to initiate a study in which we would invite first- and second-grade colleagues—Pegeen and Lisa—to join us in a collaborative examination of the effectiveness of using the writer's workshop model across grade levels. Together, we created a plan of action that included developing a longitudinal study, organizing monthly meetings, and discussing writing instruction and students' memoir writing as a benchmark unit of study.

So far in our study, we have chosen six first graders who will be engaged in writer's workshop and a memoir unit of study. We plan to group them in our classes and follow their writing progress through fourth grade. We obtained support from the principal and the speech/language teacher for help with this grouping process, and we are thinking about asking other teachers to participate in a memoir unit of study with their young writers. We surmise that children participating in this study consistently from grades 1–4 will be better writers and readers and will perform better on the fourth-grade New York State English Language Arts examination than those who do not.

MOVING FORWARD

As you continue to learn about successful collaboration, you are already beginning to collect tools and resources. Equipped with the sample timetable and teacher inquiry template from this chapter, it's time to move forward into Chapter Four, which will help you think about how to form your group and get under way. Ship ahoy!

4

Getting Started

How to Use This Chapter

You and a group of colleagues have decided to form a collaborative group to investigate a common concern. Or, as a teacher leader or administrator you want to integrate collaborative teacher research as a means of job-embedded, teacher-led professional development for your faculty. How do you go about setting up the group, establishing procedures, and determining the roles of each member for maximum efficiency and effectiveness?

This chapter provides ideas and suggestions for forming and organizing your collaborative group. It does so by presenting and describing the preliminary developmental stages for collaborative study. Groups, research needs, and situations vary widely. As your group evolves, it will move through these initial stages. One group ebbs and flows across time differently from another. After reading this chapter, apply the suggested strategies presented here to your group and its goals. Then proceed on to Chapter Five, "Staying Productive," which describes advanced stages of group development that extend the work.

Throughout the chapter, you will see references to Appendix A, "Tools and Templates," which provides reproducible forms for your group to use as they evolve through these initial stages of collaboration. The forms prompt valuable discussions that will encourage the development of positive group rapport, interaction, and efficient productivity. Throughout this chapter, figures demonstrate how members of a scenario collaborative group completed several of these forms. A description of this collaborative group is shared in this chapter in the sample scenario; examples of how this group would respond are also included to clarify each stage's progress.

INTRODUCTION

When educators who share a common goal or identity come together, they create a dynamic group that is based on the relationships, communication, values, and efforts among its members

(Vaughan & Hogg, 2002). Whether your group consists of three or ten educators, core group dynamics will exist and predict the productivity and sustainability of your group. Therefore, it is important that as a collaborative entity, you promote positive group dynamics. To do that, it is helpful to understand how a group's dynamics develop. Susan Davis Lenski offers these words about group dynamics:

> *Working in collaborative teacher research groups can be one of the most rewarding experiences an educator can have or it can be immensely frustrating. I have been involved in many collaborative projects in my career, most of them extremely rewarding. For example, for the past three years two of my colleagues and a staff member began researching how our faculty and staff describe our school's commitment to social justice. We met at noon each Tuesday at a local coffee house to develop the research project, to formulate timelines, and to analyze data. Our meetings became the highlight of the week for all of us. Not only did we conduct an interesting action research project, we became good friends.*

Some working groups end up being positive without much effort. Sometimes a good cup of coffee is all it takes. However, groups are made up of individuals who have different levels of commitment, varying demands on personal time, and a host of different reasons for becoming involved. Just as educators work toward developing positive classroom communities in which their students can learn and grow, they need to devote the same kind of attention and wisdom to the group dynamics of their teacher research group.

HOW GROUPS DEVELOP

Group development is fueled by collaboration when participants see the group as a collective force that can achieve important work that the individual members would not be able to accomplish on their own (Garmston & Wellman, 2008). Not all groups develop in exactly the same way, though. As previously stated, how a teacher research or study collaborative group grows and changes—or stagnates and dissolves—will depend on the members of the group and the situation. Are members familiar colleagues from the same school? Is your collaborative a university-school partnership? What is the length of the study? Teachers from the Saddlewood Writing Inquiry Group told us that their group was fueled by common as well as unique characteristics. They wrote that "Although the roles within our group are not defined, our years of experience, our passion for teaching writing, and our unique mixture of people who like to think 'big picture' and those who are great at looking at the details are the strengths of how the group operates."

Many factors influence the productivity and cohesiveness of a group. Several are described in Exhibit 4.1. Apply these factors to a classroom environment. One factor that highly influences how student work groups develop is how long the group will be together. When a teacher assigns group work, the groups' development depends on whether they will work together for one quick task or over an extended period of time. Undoubtedly, a teacher would consider group composition much more carefully when the groups' associations will be lengthy rather than short. The teacher knows how significantly group interactions and development over time can influence productivity and learning. Does one person take the role of leader and guide the group in industrious ways? Or does the leader control the group in destructive ways? Are members of the group encouraged to think creatively or conventionally?

The factors that influence group development are just as significant for adults in collaborative groups as they are for classroom collaborative learning. More than likely a teacher research

Exhibit 4.1: Factors That Influence Group Development

- Length of time group will work together

  Will task take ten minutes or extend over days or months?

- Whether or not group has worked together before and how successful that interaction was

  Has group already developed trust and roles? What readjustments are necessary?

- Number of people in the group

  Will everyone have an opportunity to interact and express himself?

- Makeup of the group (for example, personalities, ages, gender, status)

  Do some members carry more authority or power for some reason? How willing are people to listen actively and to consider others' perspectives?

  Who talks more?

- Trust

  Are trusting relationships forming among group members? Do members feel comfortable taking risks by expressing their thoughts freely?

- Culture

  Do culturally diverse members share common understandings about group participation, communication, roles, and norms?

Source: Adapted from Beebe & Masterson, 2000.

collaboration will work together over several months at least. (See Exhibit 3.2 for a sample timetable for a collaborative research project.) Therefore, it is important to promote positive group development. So, how do groups develop? In this chapter we will look at group dynamics in general and then apply these generalizations to the unique relationships and context of collaborative teacher research groups.

Theories of Group Development

Although there are a number of theories of group development and group psychology (for example, Bandura, 1986; Konopka, 1981; Lewin, 1948), we have found that an awareness of Tuckman's classic stages of group development (1965; Tuckman & Jensen, 1977)—forming, storming, norming, performing, and adjourning—can be helpful in sustaining productivity in collaborative teacher research groups. Let's take a quick look at each stage, then talk about how they can be applied to collaborative teacher research.

Forming   Groups are generally very polite as they get to know each other and find their position among their colleagues. Tuckman saw this stage as one in which little was achieved.

Storming   Group members start to argue with each other. Conflicts arise as members feel they are either winning or losing an argument. Suppressed arguments constrain productivity.

Norming Group members begin to acknowledge and accept each other's differences. However, they may fear expressing further differences to avoid reverting back to the storming stage.

Performing Members begin to trust each other. Tuckman saw this as the productive stage of the process in which the energy of the group can finally be aimed at achieving the group's goals; hence, the metaphor of performing.

Adjourning Members reflect upon, evaluate, acknowledge, or celebrate their accomplishments—or mourn their lack of productivity, if that be the case.

Connections to Collaborative Research and Study

Knowledge of Tuckman's stages of group development (1965; Tuckman & Jensen, 1977) provides an understanding that groups are dynamic and tend to work through a time in which they become comfortable with each other. As they become comfortable, they feel safe in taking risks and expressing ideas. This idea is supported by studies of academic group work and risk taking as well (for example, Richards, Elliott, Woloshyn, & Mitchell, 2001; Ross, Powell, & Elias, 2002). We also learn from Tuckman's work that to survive, groups need to learn to become interdependent and to work through conflicts in productive ways.

In our work with collaborative groups, we have adapted Tuckman's theory of group development (1965; Tuckman & Jensen, 1977). We base our adaptations on our observations, our experiences, and our review of current literature related to successful collaborative teacher research (for example, Burant, Gray, Ndaw, McKinney-Keys, & Allen, 2007; Mohr, Rogers, Sanford, Nocerino, MacLean, & Clawson, 2004). Although a specific situation, the group members, and the needs of the study ultimately shape group development, the following general categories characterize the development of positive, productive group dynamics within collaborative learning or research groups that extend beyond the project:

Stage 1: Getting to Know Invited Members

Stage 2: Sharing Perspectives and Talents

Stage 3: Supporting Each Other's Efforts and Learning

Stage 4: Exploring the Possibilities

Stage 5: Ongoing Conversations

Figure 4.1 illustrates each stage and its corresponding guiding questions.

THE INITIAL STAGES

As we describe each stage of collaborative teacher research group development, to help clarify the concepts involved we will compare and contrast them to Tuckman's stages. Also, we will exemplify each stage by linking it to the following scenario of an authentic group situation. When appropriate, we have applied this scenario to illustrate how this collaborative group might respond during the stage. Also, in the figures throughout this chapter, you will find samples of how this group completed several of the reproducible forms that are found in Appendix A. As you read, think about how each stage applies to your situation and study, too. This chapter will discuss the first two stages and Chapter Five will continue with Stages 3 through 5.

Stage 1: Getting to Know Invited Members
Who should be invited to be part of the group?
What are key "first discussions" to have?

Stage 2: Sharing Perspectives and Talents
What perspectives do group members offer?
What procedures will the group follow?
What roles will group members play?

Stage 3: Supporting Each Other's Efforts and Learning
How can collaborative teacher research group members
support each other in the steps of the process?

Stage 4: Exploring the Possibilities
How will the group evaluate its progress along the way?
What will become of our results and findings?
What final reflections would the group share?

Stage 5: Ongoing Conversations
What can I continue to offer my colleagues so we can develop
deeper understandings of how our study's findings apply to students?
How can I continue to learn from the expertise of my colleagues?

FIGURE 4.1. *The Dynamic Stages of a Collaborative Group*

SCENARIO

As they were talking one day about their concern with students' low test scores on the reading comprehension section of the state-mandated English Language Arts tests, Debbie, Colleen, and Mary—three fifth-grade teachers from Hilltop Elementary School—decided to take a close look at students' reading comprehension across content areas. In their school, content is departmentalized: Mary teaches science; Colleen teaches social studies; Debbie teaches reading; Reggie teaches math. Debbie, Colleen, and Mary have decided to conduct a collaborative teacher research study to systematically study students' reading comprehension progress over a three-month period from January through March. They hope to examine how students apply selected reading comprehension strategies learned in reading class to other content areas.

STAGE 1: GETTING TO KNOW INVITED MEMBERS

Stage 1 is more than the polite period in which little is achieved as Tuckman (1965; Tuckman & Jensen, 1977) suggests in his forming stage of group development. In contrast, it is a time when important decisions are being made and people gain a sense of trust and camaraderie. A collaborative culture begins to form from the melding of individuals' professional identities (Garmston & Wellman, 2008).

During Stage 1, after you've determined who to invite to join your group, you will want to raise poignant fundamental questions with members of the group to clarify important principles. See Appendix A, Form 1 for a helpful reproducible worksheet to use to brainstorm ideas for Stage 1 with your group. Exhibit 4.2 illustrates how the Hilltop teachers from the scenario responded to these questions. Also, Form 2 in Appendix A is a chart that will help you think about who could contribute to your group. The chart lists the seven steps in the teacher research process and provides spaces for you to jot down who might be able to help with each step and what he or she might contribute. For example, your school media specialist might be someone to consider for help with researching the topic for a theoretical framework (step four of the process). Use the chart to brainstorm possibilities before making final decisions. The following sections will help you think about the implications of your decisions as your group contemplates important questions.

Deciding on Group Membership

Who should be invited to be part of the group? The members of your group will be key to the success of your study. Think of your members as resources and banks of knowledge. Susan Davis Lenski advises the following:

> *Find people who are committed to the project. You will be able to find colleagues and other educators to join you if you have a well-developed purpose for your project. You should consider the different needs of each person who you want to join your group. For example, you can convince university faculty to join your research group if the outcome is a presentation or a publication. School personnel often want to see student achievement as a result. Some of your colleagues might consider using the project in graduate programs. Addressing the different needs of your group members at the outset of the project will increase their level of commitment.*

Exhibit 4.2: Scenario Example of Stage 1 as Completed by the Group Initiators—Colleen, Mary, and Debbie

Stage 1: Getting to Know Invited Members

WHO SHOULD BE INVITED TO BE PART OF THE GROUP?

1. Who can offer a certain expertise or a unique perspective to the group?

   We will want to invite the fifth-grade math, consultant special education, and the Title I reading teachers who work with our students. Our research design is quantitative and qualitative, but none of us has experience with quantitative methodology. We will ask the high school statistics teacher to join our group.

2. Who would have the time and be committed to such a project?

   Besides us, we anticipate the fifth-grade math teacher and the consultant special education teacher will be highly committed to the study. This year our Title I teacher has a heavy student load and seems overwhelmed with his current responsibilities. But we'll ask him anyway.

3. Who might act as an outside consultant or short-term advisor to the group?

   The high school statistics teacher could act as a short-term advisor when we reach that step of the research. Also, the Title I teacher may consider joining the group when we analyze the data if he cannot be a full-time member.

4. Data Collection

   a. What data will help answer the research questions?

   We plan to collect students' responses to reading, videotaped literature circle conversations around texts, standardized test scores, and interviews with students about their reading comprehension. We will each keep a research journal in which we reflect about the process and daily occurrences relating to the study and reading comprehension. Also, if the consultant and Title I teachers cannot participate as group members, we will interview them about students' progress.

   b. Who can help collect this data?

   All potential group members previously mentioned. We could also ask for help from other teachers, staff, family members, and administrators. However, these people would not be asked to be part of the core collaborative group.

5. How many members should be invited to join the group?
   To keep the group manageable and to promote effective communication, we will keep the group size to six to eight members.

WHAT ARE KEY "FIRST DISCUSSIONS" TO HAVE?

1. What do we hope to achieve from this collaboration?

(continued)

(continued)

Mutual support through a complex and important process. We think we can offer each other time, knowledge, and insight and will spark and extend each other's ideas.

2. What is our mission?

   a. What is the purpose of our group?

   To combine forces to build on each other's knowledge about theory and practice, then take that collective knowledge to study and understand how our students can best learn and integrate reading comprehension strategies.

   b. How will students benefit?

   We aim to help students improve their reading comprehension skills across the content areas.

   c. What are we doing to address this purpose?

   Our group will share articles and books about current scientifically based research, and we will conduct a systematic study.

   d. What philosophy or beliefs guide our work?

   We believe integrating explicit comprehension instruction in the curriculum across content areas and providing scaffolding and extended practice will improve students' reading comprehension.

3. How will we communicate?

   Formal, scheduled meetings and impromptu conversations.

4. Meeting Logistics and Anticipated Timetable

   a. How often will we meet?

   Formally, at least every other week to check progress. Informally, we'll have opportunities to chat daily as needed.

   b. Where?

   In one of our classrooms

   c. How long? (hours)

   Formal meetings will be at least one hour. Informal meetings, as time allows.

   d. How long do we anticipate the study will take? (number of weeks or months)

   We'll collect data for 12 weeks, discuss and analyze it for 4 weeks, then report our results. During May and June we will work on revising our curriculum to reflect our findings. Over the summer break, we hope to write up our results to be submitted to a professional journal for publication or a local conference for presentation.

5. How will we support each other throughout the process?

   Two teachers will combine study halls once per week to free one of the teachers to go into a third teacher's room to provide support for data collection. We will share articles and books, read each other's journals regularly to provide insight, and help analyze each other's data.

6. What will we do if someone has to drop out of the group?

If someone has health problems, we will work with the substitute teacher to continue data collection if possible. It wouldn't be necessary to replace the group member during the analysis and reporting steps.

When deciding group membership, we suggest that you ask yourself these questions:

1. How many members should be invited to join the group?
2. Who can offer a certain expertise, talent, or unique perspective to the group?
3. Who would have the time and ability to commit to such a project?
4. Who might act as an outside consultant or short-term advisor to the group?
5. Who can help you collect the type of data that will help answer the research question?

Each of these questions will be discussed in the following sections.

1. How many members should be invited to join the group? Though it is important to invite the people necessary to complete your study by answering your research questions with validity and reliability, you don't want your group size to be unwieldy. Noted group psychologists Beebe and Masterson (2005) recommend that groups should be small enough to encourage maximum participation, yet large enough to generate the maximum number of ideas. You don't want so many members that people don't get a chance to contribute their ideas or become passive, and you don't want it so small that the number and quality of ideas are limited. Beebe and Masterson recommend that you invite just enough people to ensure that you have all the skills you need to solve problems as they emerge. What does this mean in terms of collaborative teacher research groups?

There is no perfect number. Experts in group psychology do not even agree on a certain number. To a large extent, the size of your group will depend upon many factors, such as these:

- The number of subjects you want to involve
- The scope of the research question
- Which talents and theoretical or practical knowledge you need to tap
- The longevity of your study

In our survey of collaborative teacher research, size varied from two to seven members working on the same research question at a time. Large programs and networks, such as the Fairfax County Public Schools Teacher Researcher Network, which is highlighted in Chapter Six, include more substantial numbers of members. However, these large programs are made up of smaller school groups that work on research questions and studies relevant to their practice.

2. Who can offer a certain expertise, talent, or unique perspective to the group? Jane Hansen says this about forming groups:

To form a collaborative learning community, create a diverse group. Last year, when the third-grade teacher-researcher worried about one of her English Language Learning (ELL) students, it was the pre-

kindergarten teacher-researcher's comments about one of her ELL students that sparked the idea for what to try with the eight-year-old boy. A wide range of contributions to the conversation sparks a myriad of ideas. Within our diversity, however, we have a common interest. Throughout the last several years I have created several teams and the diverse members have always been dedicated to gaining expertise as teachers of writing.

We suggest that you be creative when thinking about whom to invite to join or consult with your group. Consider inviting a teacher from your district or a university professor who is a noted expert or who can offer unique insight into topics related to your study. Perhaps someone from your district attended a relevant conference or recently took a class at a local college and has materials or ideas to offer. Members of some students' families might lend a unique perspective or talent to your group, too. They see how students apply what they are learning in school to nonacademic settings. They also may be able to offer their time during the day to help collect or organize data. When it comes to data analysis and interpretation, you might want to ask outside speech and language, special education, literacy, or other specialists and consultant teachers to help you interpret or even collect data. Try contacting teachers from multiple grade levels both preceding and following yours to provide insight about curriculum, skills, or particular students' progress. Ask teaching assistants and administrators when appropriate. The idea is to keep an open mind and think creatively about who might be able to provide valuable insight, talents, or perspectives. The amount of energy, resourcefulness, and groundedness that each member brings to the collaboration will develop the synergy of the group (Garmston & Wellman, 2008).

3. Who would have the time and ability to commit to such a project? Let's face it. We are all busy, and there are not enough hours in the day. This project is a long-term commitment.

Select people who are genuinely interested and passionate about your project and are willing to make it a priority and commit a certain amount of time and energy. Be realistic about the amount of time each member will be committing to even before beginning the project. Make it clear during your initial invitation exactly what part each member will play. Stress that each person will have a specific supporting part and that the success of the study depends on each member fulfilling his or her obligation to the group. In the end, though, have a plan of action to compensate for a member who ultimately must unexpectedly drop out of the study before it is complete. Just as we overcompensate when selecting study participants for our research in case a student moves out of the school district, we should set up our collaborative research group with the idea that sometimes even the most committed and reliable people are offered new jobs or have other issues that prevent them from completing their commitment. This is a potential issue particularly in longitudinal studies that extend over several years. During a recent study that Cindy was involved in, a key person was offered a new position in the second year of the study. This person had contributed pivotal talents to the group. However, we were able to continue the study because we had used preventative measures: we already had another instructor to fulfill her contributions.

4. Who might act as an outside consultant or short-term advisor to the group? Not all members have to be full-time participants. You may want to invite an expert in a certain type of data analysis to consult with your group when it is time to work with data. In Cindy's department, one colleague is very familiar and knowledgeable about analyzing quantitative data using computer software. He is helpful when it comes to that part of the study. However, another colleague is talented in recognizing themes or patterns across the data. If a colleague has a particular strength that you would like to include in your work but he or she cannot make an extended commitment, consider inviting him or her to join the group at a key time. Keep track of these limited participants and their contribution to your group's work. You will want to acknowledge their participation when you speak or write about your study. Also, you will want to send a formal letter of appreciation and ask whether the person would like a letter sent to a supervisor.

5. Who can help you collect the type of data that will help answer the research question?

To answer the research question, you will want to collect several types of data. Who is in a position to collect valuable data for your study? For example, in our scenario, the group wants to ask the consultant teachers who work with their students to join their group. They feel that these teachers can provide insight into the students' learning processes and contextual factors influencing students' production. Both consultant teachers are brought or "pushed" into the classrooms to coteach with the classroom teacher. Therefore, they are readily available to collect valuable data.

Keep in mind that it isn't mandatory to invite particular colleagues who are in a position to collect data, such as students' work samples, to join the group in order to use student work samples generated during their instructional time with a student. You could still ask these teachers to share students' work with you for your study, and you could interview the teacher about his or her work with the students. Determine whether or not to ask potential data collectors to join the group based on combined responses to other questions in this section.

Setting Collaboration Ground Rules

Once members are invited and assembled, you will need to have straightforward, honest conversations that open possibilities for the group. Right from the start, let it be known that everyone's ideas are welcome and encouraged. A group's interactions, interdependence, and caring for each other and the group inspire members to remain committed to the work and each other (Garmston & Wellman, 2008). What are the ground rules for the collaboration?

Group psychologists (Katzenbach & Smith, 2003; Scholtes, Joiner, & Streibel, 2003) teach us that high-performing groups are effective because they set and discuss clear ground rules, or explicit, collectively accepted norms for acceptable and unacceptable behavior. These ground rules should reflect the group's values.

Ground rules for collaborative teacher research groups may include

- What a member should do if he or she cannot attend a meeting
- How the group will manage conflict among members
- How decisions will be made (for example, by consensus rather than by a vote)
- Expectations for members' promptness and preparedness for meetings
- Expectations for following up on responsibilities between meetings
- Expectations for ethical and fair treatment of colleagues and study participants

Deciding on a Mission

A mission statement describes the goals and desired outcomes of the collaboration (Beebe & Masterson, 2005). Forming a mission statement helps clarify the group's collective thoughts and intentions into one concise statement. The existence of the statement is useful because members can continually look back at it to evaluate whether the direction of the group stays on course or is evolving. For example, the group in our scenario refers to their mission statement when they approach each step of the teacher research process (such as identifying the inquiry, designing the research plan, collecting the data, and so forth). They find it helps clarify and evaluate their main purpose for the collaboration. Sometimes, as a study progresses and weeks and months pass, it is beneficial to revisit the mission statement to regain focus and to see if or how the purpose or goals of the research may be evolving.

In framing your mission statement, you will aim to describe the nature, values, and work of the collaboration. Recommendations differ regarding what a mission statement should specifically include. Select from the following list of questions, created by combining our experiences with the work of Radtke (1998) and Covey (2004), to write a concise mission statement for your group.

a. What is the purpose of our group? (Radtke, 1998)

b. What are we doing to address this purpose? (Radtke, 1998)

c. What measures will we take to ensure ethics are maintained? (Israel & Lassonde, 2008)

d. How will students benefit from this collaborative teacher research?

e. What philosophy or beliefs guide our work? (Radtke, 1998)

f. How will we measure if our goals have been achieved? (Covey, 2004)

g. How will our findings guide our practice?

h. How will we share our findings to benefit other colleagues and students?

You may find your group does not need to address all of these questions at this time. You may decide to revisit your statement and add to or revise it as your group becomes more active and involved in your research. See Exhibit 4.2 under "What is our mission?" for the initial mission statement written by the sample scenario group.

Planning to Convene the Group

Discuss the options for communication. Perhaps everyone in your group works in the same school building. You can schedule formal face-to-face meetings on a regular basis, and plan to touch base with each other more frequently as questions or problems arise, meeting in a classroom after school or in the faculty room during lunch. However, if members are scattered among buildings or schedules don't allow impromptu meetings between the scheduled ones, you could plan conference calls or e-mail communication. There are other online communication systems available, too, such as blogs and Google groups that many researchers are using to communicate across distances and time. These methods are valuable because they fit the needs of our busy schedules.

How often will we meet face-to-face? Where? How long? You will find that meeting frequency will vary depending on which stage of group development, the duration and complexity of your study, and on which teacher research step you are working. (See Falk-Ross and Cuevas's [2008] steps of teacher research in Chapter Three.) In the beginning steps, you will want to meet frequently enough that members feel comfortable expressing themselves, know their roles, are clear about the group's mission and goals, and know the procedures. Weekly meetings might be in order for the first month as the group forms the research question and designs the study. It is important for everyone to understand who is responsible for what and when so that you can avoid missed opportunities to, for example, collect or save data.

Once the study is designed and you are collecting and organizing data, you will want to meet regularly to review the procedure and discuss themes you see emerging from the data as the study progresses. In our survey, respondents said they met at least monthly. We have found in our own work that a combination of formal meetings and apropos conversations and e-mails help keep everyone abreast of what is going on.

Near the end of the study, when you are determining the results and planning ways to share your findings, you may find it helpful to again meet more frequently than once a month. Letting your data sit for too long may make the context of its creation more distant in memory. For example, if you are using students' work samples as data, the context of the writing situation may be very important to your study. Was the sample written in a writer's workshop, a small group, or individually? Was there a writing prompt? What kind of feedback or direction was provided during the writing?

Sometimes, unexpected problems arise that require either a quick response or an additional meeting. Even if not all members can schedule in these unanticipated meetings, you can share the notes from the meetings and ask for absent members' responses. Allow your meetings to be flexible to account for additional support and discussion as needed.

Following are some thoughts about meetings from Jane Hansen:

Create a consistent schedule to meet often and regularly. My current team meets at a coffee shop, and the shop owners know us as the Monday Night Teachers. These meetings are as imprinted on our calendars as the dates and times of our other learning and teaching responsibilities.

My current group meets every week. In the past some groups I have been a part of met every other week. Another group, larger than my current group, included a portion of people who couldn't meet every week, so the rest met every week and the portion joined every other week. All variations work. Personally, I have been a member of groups for more than two decades and none of them has ever met less frequently than every other week. Our conversations flow from meeting to meeting; we can remember the students we talk about!

Where a group meets—some of my former groups met in classrooms or homes—doesn't matter, what matters is to find a space that works. When a group meets—many of my former groups have met after school—doesn't matter, what matters is to find a time that accommodates all members.

My current group meets for 1½ hours. Previous groups have met for an hour. I think the length of the time period depends on the tasks or format the group creates. Regardless, it is very important to start and end on time. We lead busy, complicated lives; and we manage to survive when we build some predictability into them. We know when our meetings end.

During the days between our meetings, the doctoral students and I each collect data in a classroom twice a week, in the form of field notes that we record as the teacher teaches, and as we interact or confer with the students while they write. Plus, we photocopy students' work to accompany our notes. The teacher-researchers keep notes in their own varied ways and photocopy students' work that exemplifies their notes.

Maintaining and Sustaining Group Membership

What will we do if someone has to drop out of the group? Bringing this question up during first conversations with the group may seem futile because sometimes there is no viable answer. Realistically, sometimes when a key member of the group has to leave for one reason or another (for example, changing positions, health reasons, or taking on new obligations that restrict the amount of time the person can meaningfully contribute to the group), the group becomes unproductive and the project doesn't succeed. There are several ways to attempt to prevent this from happening.

First, try to prevent it ahead of time. Invite group members who are most likely to commit seriously to your project. Be realistic about who is reputable for following through on his commitments to projects such as this. Who would be beneficial to have on the team but seems already overwhelmed with responsibilities? Consider who might join your group as a core member who participates from initiation to finish and who might be invited to join for a short time to offer a certain expertise. Notice how the scenario group answered this question. They noted that they would like to ask the Title I person, but they realized he was scheduled to have a heavy workload this year. When they approach him, they must be sure to discuss issues of accountability to the group if he decides to join. Stressing the importance of consistency, commitment, and accountability are necessary when inviting members.

Next, ask each member of the group to provide a response to this question:

If I cannot continue with the project, how could the group replace my contribution?

By asking each member to provide an answer, you not only are stressing the importance of his accountability to the group and his contribution, but you are creating a list of problem-solving solutions directly connected to each person's potential absence. Some solutions might involve finding a replacement, restructuring the design of the study to accommodate for the group's loss, or revising the research question. For example, if Mary unexpectedly had to leave the school and the group, someone could take over her responsibilities to the group (such as her substitute teacher, the other group members, other teachers or staff) or the question could be revised to exclude science class because that is what Mary taught. If the high school statistics teacher had to drop out of the group and you couldn't find a replacement, you could exclude the use of quantitative methods, or someone else in the group could learn how to calculate it.

Finally, what happens if there is no possible solution to replacing the member's contributions to the group? Does the study automatically end? Sometimes major adjustments must be made or the study must be cut short. However, the time already invested in the project should not have to go to waste. Valuable data may already be collected that can be used to answer part of your research question. In some cases, the study may be used as a pilot study. A pilot study is a trial, usually a smaller-scale study that can provide valuable information that leads to the larger-scale study being more organized and successful. In the case of our scenario, the Hillside group could conduct a pilot study of how students' reading comprehension was influenced by a particular method within one content area. They could use the same research design and methodology they intend to use in the larger study before delving into the more comprehensive study that extends across content areas. This way they could use the pilot study as a trial run to see if the intended design needs revision. So, for example, if Colleen, the social studies teacher, had to drop out of the study, the data collected in another content area with only one class of students could still be used to do a smaller study.

STAGE 2: SHARING PERSPECTIVES AND TALENTS

In Tuckman's model (1965), conflicts were seen as initially disruptive but eventually necessary to a group's production. In our model, we prefer to use the term *sharing perspectives*. The word *conflicts* denotes a negative confrontation that people hope to avoid. An important component of collaborative teacher research is the gathering of people who offer different ideas that will stir up thoughts, invigorate options to consider, and provide background knowledge. For example, educators come to the group with different experiences in teaching, philosophy, and education. Sharing perspectives is a means for discussing these diverse experiences and acknowledging commonalities. However, perhaps most important, it is a means of learning from each other. During this stage of group development, members should ask the following questions. (See Appendix A, Form 3.)

Clarifying Perspectives That Group Members Offer

Research is all about asking questions, inquiring, analyzing, and interpreting data. Multiple perspectives presented in professional tones become welcomed insights to fill in each other's gaps of knowledge and experience. Therefore, in collaborative teacher research, Tuckman's storming and norming stages (1965) become invigorating brainstorming sessions. Brainstorming allows participants to work toward solutions to problems by creating new ideas. Through brainstorming techniques, judgment is suspended as participants generate new ideas through free association. Possibilities are explored and sought rather than looked upon as disruptions. In a brainstorming session, there are no wrong responses. All participants are encouraged to say whatever comes to mind in a safe, unbiased environment. It is amazing sometimes how stray comments can sometimes lead to divergent thinking and creative solutions during brainstorming sessions.

Besides brainstorming methods, participants should feel comfortable asking questions and sharing their knowledge and understandings. It may feel awkward at first to express a contradictory viewpoint or to question a colleague's understanding of a topic, but this is something that should be encouraged in collaborative teacher research. We have found in groups with which we work that a collective body of knowledge exists among members. This body of knowledge grows as members open communication channels and share their perceptions. Read how Debbie opens up to Reggie's perceptions about a piece of data in the following conversation.

Debbie: (looking at a transcript of a videotaped conversation with a student) Right here, when Tomas says, "I know what all the words mean so it's easy to understand it," he is saying that knowing the vocabulary ensures a reader's comprehension.

Reggie: I've read that there are different levels of knowing a word, though. And just because he says he understands the passage, we can't assume he does. While I think vocabulary is key to comprehension—does a reader have to know all the words to understand a passage? I think there are lots of factors to consider here before we try to interpret what Tomas is saying.

Debbie: I think we should do some follow-up with Tomas and ask him what he meant when he said that. And could you find more information about the different levels of knowing vocabulary to show me? I'd like to read more about that.

Note how Reggie adds his understanding of levels of vocabulary from what he has read elsewhere to his conversation with Debbie. What a valuable contribution! He not only shared his knowledge but also provided a new perspective for Debbie to consider when he asks whether readers have to know all the words to understand a passage. This discussion has the potential to lead to further reading and deeper understanding of reading comprehension and vocabulary development that will result in more effective teaching and learning. This wouldn't have happened without the collaboration.

Besides offering various perspectives about interpreting data and knowledge about theories and practices, members may contribute insight into diverse cultural and learning perspectives and needs.

Look to members of the group who have experience with multicultural environments and readings to shed light on some subjects' perceptions. Look to those with experience and knowledge of students with special needs to provide insight on diverse learning approaches and needs.

Meeting Procedures

When a teacher research group works together, members should establish procedures for the meetings. Draw upon the talents of group members to organize the meetings in a manner that allows for the most efficient use of everyone's time. Here are some suggestions you will find helpful in setting group proceedings.

A Group Folder   One designated member of the group should maintain a group file folder in which he or she keeps a copy of all group correspondences and notes (such as the tentative agendas, final agendas, and minutes). This folder should be available to all members for review. Bring the folder to all meetings in case you need to refer to any notes.

A Group Agenda   About one week before the scheduled meeting, one designated member of the group should distribute a completed tentative agenda that itemizes topics to be discussed at the upcoming meeting. (See Exhibit 4.3 and Appendix A, Form 4). It also acts to remind everyone there is an upcoming meeting. Fill in items you already know should take place and leave sections blank for others to insert their agenda items—the concerns they want to bring up at the meeting. Distribute the tentative agenda to all members and keep one copy for the group file. Ask members to add to or revise the agenda prior to the day of the meeting (give them a specific due date by which to respond) if there is anything in particular they want to discuss. The agenda becomes the skeleton outline for the meeting. Its purpose is to keep everyone on task and to make the best use of everyone's time. The agenda is a detailed list of items the group feels are important and doesn't want to forget to bring up at the meeting.

The meeting will begin with a review and approval of the minutes from the previous meeting and a quick group evaluation activity (described more fully later in Stage 3), so these items are noted. Then the agenda may begin with a section on "old business," which devotes time to following up on items discussed at the latest meeting and acted upon between meetings. Next, a "new business" section could list current items. We suggest you prioritize items in this section based on what absolutely must be discussed for timely reasons related to the design of the study (high-priority topics), quick clarifying questions members have, important topics, and low-priority topics. Then, if time runs short because an item needed in-depth discussion before proceeding, at least the project can still move on. Finally, the "actions to take" and "scheduling of next meeting" headings are included on the agenda but not filled in prior to the meeting. They appear on the agenda just as a reminder that they will be decided at the meeting.

At each meeting, every member should be given a copy of the updated agenda, which has been revised to include any new items that members have requested. As the meeting progresses, be mindful of the amount of items to be discussed and the length of the meeting. Devote appropriate amounts of time to each item. At the end of the meeting, review what action(s) will be taken before the next meeting and who is responsible for it. Then, schedule the date, time, and place for the next meeting. Base the interval between meetings on the group's needs for support of the other members and the teacher research step on which you are working, as described previously.

Exhibit 4.3: Sample Agenda

(Note that some areas are left blank for group members prior to the finalization of the agenda to insert concerns they want to bring up at the meeting.)

TO: *Mary, Reggie, Debbie*

Tentative Agenda for *Wednesday, September 17th* Meeting

Place: *Mary's classroom*

Time: *3 PM to 4 PM*

Please review the following agenda. If you want to add anything or make any revisions to it, please let me know by *Monday, September 15th* by *e-mailing me at my school address.* Thank you.

Connie L. at conniel@hilltopschool.com

Review and Approval of Minutes

_____
_____
_____

Quick Group Evaluation

_____
_____
_____

Old Business

_____
_____

Follow-up items: *Finish our discussion about think-alouds (see the article by Schoenbach et al.); how does this apply to us?*

Reports of action taken since last meeting: *Debbie will report on what she found out about getting some books on comprehension through the Teacher's Center funding.*

New Business

_____
_____

High-priority items: *We planned to read through students' science lab notebooks so we could talk about them this week.*

Quick questions: *What data have we collected since last meeting?*

Important items

Low-priority items

(continued)

(*continued*)

Actions to Take

_____

_____

_____

Scheduling of Next Meeting

_____

_____

_____

Meeting Minutes Who will take notes or minutes during the meeting? One group member should be responsible for recording the group's progress each time it meets. It is most efficient if the person taking the minutes can do so on a computer (laptop) during the meeting. The minutes should list which members were present, summarize decisions that were made, describe answers provided to group members, and note what actions will be taken and who is responsible for each action. Finally, the minutes should include information about the next scheduled meeting or plans for communication. (See Exhibit 4.4 for sample minutes and Appendix A, Form 5 for a blank

Exhibit 4.4: Sample Meeting Minutes

Date of Meeting *9-17-09*

Meeting Began *3 PM* (time)

Meeting Ended *4 PM* (time)

Members Present: *Connie, Mary, Reggie, Debbie*

Members Absent:

These Items Were Discussed	Actions to Be Taken and by Whom
We need more articles on the effectiveness of using multiple comprehension strategies.	*Connie will ask librarian for help with interlibrary loans to get articles.*
Science labs seem to indicate outlines are more effective with striving readers than text highlighting.	*Mary will research and bring in more info on using outlines.*
Reggie was worried about having enough time to interview individual students.	*Debbie and Mary will cover his study hall next week so he can talk with and tape students.*

Next meeting will be on *Wed., 9-28-09* (date) at *3 PM* (time) in *elementary library* (where)

minutes form.) Distribute the minutes to each group member, being especially sure that absent members receive a copy. If minutes were taken on a computer during the meeting, they can easily be e-mailed to each group member through a distribution list, saving time, energy, and resources. Otherwise, minutes should be copied and distributed to members in a timely fashion. Then everyone has record of who is doing what before the next meeting.

CLARIFYING ROLES THAT GROUP MEMBERS WILL PLAY

Members will be able to contribute special talents and skills related to being researchers and being group supporters. These talents will lend themselves to playing certain roles in the group. At one of your first meetings, when you have everyone who will be involved in the collaboration gathered, describe each of the roles below and ask people for which they would like to be responsible. A sample signup sheet appears in Exhibit 4.5, and a blank sheet can be found in Appendix A, Form 6.

Susan Davis Lenski offers the following about group roles:

First, appoint a convener and chief worrier. If you have initiated the project, you might want to be "in charge." Most groups need someone who will convene meetings and be the overall person who is a leader. Some groups function well by rotating leadership, but most groups need to have one person who makes arrangements for meetings, who makes sure to get the appropriate approvals, and who can be relied on to know answers to various questions. Next, define roles and responsibilities. Many groups function best when each member has distinct roles and responsibilities. You might want to list the kinds of activities that the group will engage in and have group members volunteer for different roles. These roles should be defined at one of the early meetings, written down, and distributed to all group members.

Exhibit 4.5: Sample Group Roles Signup Sheet

Role	Duties	Responsible Member(s)
Group Leader	Convene group; overall voice and contact person for group	*Connie*
Group Recordkeeper	Organize and maintain data files	*Debbie*
Group Recorder	Agenda and minutes	*Mary*
Group Research Checker(s)	Scope out scientifically based research on a topic as needed	*Mary*
Group Teacher Research Expert(s)	Resource for how to go about doing teacher research	*Debbie*
Group Conflict Resolver(s)	Act as mediators	*Reggie*
Group Evaluator(s)	Ongoing evaluation; report to group	*Connie*
Other Experts:		
Qualitative Data Analysis		*Reggie*

In the following sections, we outline some specific roles members may take on.

Group Leader

Usually awarded to the person or people initiating the group, the group leader is the "go-to" person who organizes other roles and overall meeting procedures. The group leader may not be the most powerful or knowledgeable person in the group or even lead the conversations in the meetings. The leader would be the person or people to keep administrators abreast of what the group is doing and otherwise act as the public relations person who answers for and promotes the group's actions. Earlier, Susan Davis Lenski referred to this person as the "convener and chief worrier."

Group Recordkeeper

One or two people should be in charge of keeping the data and the group correspondence (for example, agendas, minutes, and so on) neatly filed and secure. At any time, any group member should be able to go to the group recordkeeper and retrieve a piece of data with ease. All data should be described in a data journal and dated and logged into a data log appropriately organized to meet the needs of the study. See Tables 4.1 and 4.2 for examples of data collection records for the scenario study. Note a separate log sheet would be identified for each content area, and data samples would be identified by content area and sequence.

Group Recorder

This person or people are in charge of the agenda and minutes. This role could be shared and rotated from meeting to meeting, or it could remain the responsibility of one person.

Group Research Checker

One or two people who have experience in searching for and finding research related to a topic and have access to a computer and academic library should be identified as the group's research

TABLE 4.1. *Data Journal Sample*

	Science Data			
Sample Number & Date	**Type**	**Prompt**	**Other Context**	**Initial Analysis**
SS1—9-10	Pretest— electricity	Write what you know about electricity.	Students were given 10 minutes. Most were done in 6–7 minutes.	Responses were less scientific than common knowledge.
SS2—9-13	Reading #1	Take notes on what you read.	Used passage from textbook, p. 13. See sample attached.	Notes were brief summaries of definitions. No connections made to experience or other readings.

TABLE 4.2. *Data Log Sample*

Student's Code	Science Data			
	SS1—9/10	SS2—9/13	SS3—9/13	SS4—9/17
1	X	X	X	X
2	X	absent	absent	X
3	X	X	X	X
4	X	X	X	X
5	X	X	X	X
6	X	X	X	X
7	X	X	X	X
8	X	X	X	X
9	X	X	X	X
10	X	X	X	X
11	X	X	X	absent
12	X	X	X	X

checkers. During meetings, when members question what the literature says about a certain topic, the checkers would be assigned to scope out relevant articles and books to bring back to the group.

Group Teacher Research Expert

One or two people who have experience in conducting teacher research should be identified as the group's experts in this area. When questions arise about the steps of teacher research, these experts would share their knowledge and bring in additional information and resources as needed.

Conflict Resolvers

One or two people who the group feels have a reputation for being fair mediators should be identified as the conflict resolvers. Members who feel uncomfortable with another member should go to the resolvers for help. Issues that arise should be discussed at the next meeting or privately among those concerned, as appropriate. The resolvers should treat the matter tactfully, honestly, and ethically.

Group Evaluators

Two or more people should be in charge of ongoing evaluation of the group's progress. Suggestions for embedded evaluation are discussed in Stage 4.

Other Experts

You will want to identify other experts as well, so the group knows ahead of time whom to go to with a specific question. For example, if your research is related to reading comprehension as our scenario is, who knows most about this area? If you are using a quantitative methodology, who is an expert in statistics?

Identifying roles and experts in advance can save the group time and effort in the long run. Rather than having members who lack expertise in an area trying to track down answers, these experts will have the answers or at least know where to find the answers. They are more likely to have helpful resources at their fingertips. If these experts are identified, members can contact them between meetings when they have specific questions, rather than having to delay progress by waiting until the next meeting. In group discussions, these people can facilitate conversations that lead to group understandings of concepts and processes. For instance, when discussing teacher research, members will have different experiences with and understandings of what it is and what the process entails. The group teacher research experts can bring in resources and readings for the group, then lead a discussion to form a collective understanding of how the group is going to define the process.

Next, Susan Davis Lenski offers the wisdom of her extensive work in collaborative learning communities and shares the following thoughts about managing time in a group to craft positive working groups.

THINKING TOGETHER: MANAGING TIME

Contributed by Susan Davis Lenski

DEVELOP A FIRM BUT FLEXIBLE TIMELINE

It is easy for time to slip away from all of us, so having a timeline of activities is beneficial for most people. There are some deadlines that need to be firm, such as when you intend to begin collecting data. There are other deadlines, such as writing the project for publication, that should remain somewhat flexible so that individuals can complete their work according to their own schedules.

RESPECT ALL FORMS OF PARTICIPATION

One of the difficulties with group work is that not everyone will contribute equally. Know that each group member will participate in different ways and respect everyone's contributions.

FOCUS ON THE WORK, NOT THE PERSONALITIES

During many research projects, tensions arise and tempers fray. If you focus on meeting agreed-on timelines and remember the purpose of the research, you'll be more inclined to remain positive. It's important to protect your relationships with your colleagues during the tough times of your project.

CELEBRATE MILESTONES

Conducting teacher research is exhilarating, but it can be a long process. When you finish a component of your research, such as getting district approval or completing data collection, celebrate by giving everyone a thank-you note or bringing a snack to your next meeting.

COLLABORATION AT WORK

Creating Consistency

Contributed by Jane Hansen

Overall, the reasons my various collaborative communities have worked are: We enjoy being together! We know each other. I maintain a rolling membership; each year some of the members continue from the previous year and some are new. We meet regularly and frequently. All of us come to our meetings prepared, ready to learn, and—for certain—ready to talk!

With this knowledge of what makes our community work, I keep in mind these three considerations each year:

- I gather a group of passionate educators whose *contributions* will be diverse. The life-saving feature of collaborative learning communities is diversity. It promises new, unexpected ideas. These collaborations become closely knit groups; that's when real talk happens.

In my current group our talk represents diverse perspectives. One of us approaches from the stance of critical pedagogy, one of us has a master's degree in math education, and one of us is addicted to film. It's important to note that none of us likes to teach—we all love it—for our own reasons.

- The leader has the crazy task of reining in this diverse group! In my group, that is my task and the six tease me—laugh at me!—whenever I stop a conversation and call on someone else to read their contribution. Just as if I'm teaching third grade! They know, however, how vital this *consistency* is. We have all come prepared, and we will each be in the spotlight for our own few minutes.

Plus, knowing that we do this every single week at the same time at the same place with the same people creates the safety we need to be able to honestly write about our teaching and our students as learners.

- Consistency contributes to the quality of our talk, our *commentary*, at our meetings. Frequently, participants comment on these collaborative gatherings as the most significant professional development they engage in.

Even though I regulate the time of the group, and I am the one who created this current, ongoing group (ongoing, but morphing from year to year), I do not run the meetings. I do not control the conversation. I do not dominate the talk. I am not the first to respond after each person reads. I am a part of the talk, but my role during talk time is the same as that of everyone else.

A group must have a leader, but it must not even occur to that leader to want to control the group. The comments belong to the group, to all. All voices find an honored space.

IS COLLABORATION RIGHT FOR ME?

Thinking ahead is always recommended, especially when it comes to entering into a commitment with colleagues. We end this chapter about the initial stages of group development by asking you to consider, now that you know more about forming a group and sharing perspectives, where you fit into the collaboration picture. Before leaping into a collaborative team, read the following Thinking Together contribution by Christine Mallozzi. Ask yourself the questions she poses to determine if collaboration is right for you at this time or in this particular situation.

THINKING TOGETHER: IS COLLABORATION RIGHT FOR ME?

Contributed by Christine Mallozzi

Many hands make light work, except when it comes to collaborative teacher research. In splitting up the tasks of a collaborative project, one may assume each person has less to do, but research is not always quantifiably divisible among collaborators. The qualities of collaborative tasks often become more intense, masking that people are sharing the work. Intensity is not bad, but it can take collaborators by surprise. Researchers may not anticipate the challenges, beauty, and rewards of a collaborative project, so entering a collaborative teacher research project is a step to be made thoughtfully. Before taking that step, no harm exists in asking "Is this the right way to go?" I invite you to ask a few more questions of yourself before you leap into a collaborative project.

CAN I STUMBLE THEN STEADY MYSELF?

No doubt, collaborative teacher-researchers do not always walk a smooth and safe path. Keeping eyes on a common goal can be consuming, making it easy to forget to look for uneven ground. Each collaborator brings individual expertise to the project, so even in a cooperative atmosphere, each researcher has a different research cache. Not all researchers are working on equal footing. In fact, collaborative teacher research is often designed to unsettle researchers and to call current practices and beliefs into question, so they can be refined. Teachers who open their classrooms for critique are putting themselves at risk, but those who are willing to critique are also at risk for having their opinions disregarded by other experts. All collaborators expose themselves and must be willing to negotiate an uneven path, so that the fear of a misstep does not paralyze the process. Collaborators must believe they can steady themselves in this work.

WILL I ACCEPT A HELPING HAND?

In a collaborative teacher research project, no one researcher can negotiate all the issues, and no one researcher is expected to. Even if collaborative researchers believe they can steady themselves, collaboration involves entertaining the notion that someone else may be better able to help you than you can help yourself. Accepting help when fumbling with a tough issue is not simple. One person may need to lead the others in knowledge, passion, or vision until they can contribute their own gifts. Shared decision making can be difficult, but when researchers are "down," it can be tempting for another researcher to yank everyone upright and sprint to make up the pace. A level of trust needs to be cultivated and maintained so that one researcher will not take the hands of the others and drag them along uncomfortably. That trust also needs to work so that one researcher can guide *with the willing support of others, allowing everyone to move in the same direction without misgivings.*

How Thin Is My Skin?

Being conscious of one's research "skin" may never be as important as when a researcher enters into a collaborative project. It's a Goldilocks issue of having skin that is not too thick, not too thin, but just right. The assertion of collaborative teacher research is that current practices are not as strong as they could be. Teacher researchers may infer they and their classrooms are subpar. Collaborative researchers may recognize their research methodology and implementation are entirely effective in an on-site classroom. These inclinations can be translated to insults, but researchers need to have a thick enough skin to sustain evaluation of the process and their roles in it. Equally, collaborators need to have thin enough skins to be sensitive to the opportunities for improvement that the research offers. Thin skins allow researchers to be aware of how others are faring and to progress gingerly, if needed. Proceeding with a combination of courage and caution can prevent the sting of scraped egos.

Am I Raw with Theory?

Working with others does not mean that everyone needs to see the world in exactly the same way. The research project needs to have a clear theoretical approach from the outset so all members of the team can work with this theory in mind. However, not all collaborators may see that particular theory as the guideline for life. This can pose a difficulty. When there are personal theoretical differences among researchers, feelings can get hurt unknowingly. Theory can act like salt in a wound, a reminder that collaboration with others is too hard or too problematic right now. This rawness can delay moving on with collaborative research until the ache is gone. On the other hand, theory can also be a bandage; maybe the hurt exists, but theorizing over the incident can provide solace, fodder for more research, and a way to move on with the research for the moment. A researcher may decide to divorce personal theoretical leanings from the project's theory or decide to work only with others who have the same worldview and do work in that vein. Both have their limitations, but a researcher's ability to temper the rawness of theory and tolerate its complexities may make a difference in a collaborative research project.

If your answers to these questions nudge you away from a collaborative teacher research project, it does not mean you are never meant to conduct collaborative teacher research. It may mean that current circumstances regarding a particular project do not fit your needs as a researcher. "No for now" may be your best response. For every research project you accept that does not suit your needs, less time exists for other work that may truly move you. The pressure to be in constant motion with research may make researchers feel like they should wait for a more optimal project, but waiting time can provide the space to develop and improve a research project to better suit the needs of collaborators. Instead of asking "Is collaborative teacher research the right way to go?" ask "Is this the right way to go—right for me, right now?" Doing so will allow you to answer no with generosity and yes with commitment.

WHAT IS NEXT?

You're on your way! In this chapter you learned about Stages 1 and 2 of the categories that characterize the development of positive, productive group dynamics within collaborative learning or research groups. In Chapter Five, you will read about the remaining stages and how to apply them in your collaborations.

5

Staying Productive

How to Use This Chapter

In Chapter Four you acquired ideas and suggestions for forming and organizing your collaborative group. Once your group is formed, how do you maintain relationships and foster a rich context for productive collaboration over time? This chapter provides information that will help support and maintain your collaborative group once it is up and running. Also, you will gain resources and ideas for reflecting upon and extending your community's interactions and productivity. In addition, we present more advanced developmental stages of group dynamics. After reading this chapter, adapt and apply the suggested strategies presented here to your group and its goals.

Throughout the chapter, you will see references to Appendix A, which provides reproducible forms for your group to use as they evolve through these extended stages of collaboration. The forms prompt valuable discussions that will encourage the development of positive group rapport, interaction, and efficient productivity. We also refer to the scenario collaborative group introduced in Chapter Four to embed processes within a specific context. This practice helps to clarify the collaborative process.

INTRODUCTION

To refresh your memory from Chapter Four, in our work with collaborative groups we have adapted Tuckman's theory of group development (1965; Tuckman & Jensen, 1977). The following stages reflect our adaptation:

Stage 1: Getting to Know Invited Members

Stage 2: Sharing Perspectives and Talents

Stage 3: Supporting Each Other's Efforts and Learning

Stage 4: Exploring the Possibilities

Stage 5: Ongoing Conversations

Remember to refer to Chapter Four, which discusses Stages 1 and 2 in detail. Also, Figure 4.1 illustrates Stages 1 through 5 and their corresponding guiding questions. This chapter will focus on Stages 3 through 5 to help you support and extend your group's work together.

STAGE 3: SUPPORTING EACH OTHER'S EFFORTS AND LEARNING

In collaborative teacher research, everyone should feel like they own the project. As a result of each member's contributions, the project reflects everyone's efforts. Therefore, when a member needs support, other members should offer their time, knowledge, and insight to assist. In Chapter Four we noted how Tuckman (1965; Tuckman & Jensen, 1977) refers to this stage in his model as Performing. Members have formed trusting relationships and are focused on working on mutual goals.

Collaboratively Shaping the Study

To fully understand how Stage 3 fits into the teacher research process and collaborative learning communities, let's look at Falk-Ross and Cuevas's steps of teacher research (2008) listed in Chapter Three. We will think about examples of how groups can support each other through their development of their study. As you read, apply these ideas to your group and to the scenario group from Chapter Four.

Identifying the Inquiry   Some groups come together already knowing the inquiry; it is the reason they came together in the first place. Other groups come with a general desire to do research to inform and improve their practice and students' learning. In these cases members work together to identify what they want to study. Group members can list topics they are interested in researching, share and discuss them, and determine common concerns.

Developing Purposes and Potential Research Questions for the Study   Research questions sometimes evolve as a study progresses. In a collaborative group, questions may be expanded to include multiple contexts. For example, in the scenario in Chapter Four, each content-area teacher will look at reading comprehension development within their subject. They will each learn about how students learn reading comprehension strategies within the teacher's content area, but collectively they will also learn about the processes involved in students' learning to comprehend what they read as they support each other's data collection and analysis.

Researching the Topic for a Theoretical Framework   Once the questions are determined, the group can decide which theories and readings will frame their study. Then, group members can search out related readings to share with the group. One meeting can be devoted to discussing the readings. The group member who provided the readings can act as the facilitator for the conversation related to his or her reading.

Designing and Organizing a Research Plan   Here is where your experts will help. The strength of your collaboration lies in inviting members who offer their special talents. Rely on your teacher research and other special experts when designing your research plan.

Collecting, Organizing, and Analyzing Data This is where the practicality of collaboration really comes in handy. As teacher researchers, it can be difficult to be in charge of twenty-five students while trying to collect data by videotaping a small group or interviewing an individual student. In a collaborative group, you should be able to count on your colleagues to support you by scheduling times to help each other with data collection. In our scenario, the members plan to combine study halls occasionally so a teacher can be free to spend time in another teacher's room. This can allow the teacher time to organize data, interview students, or catch up in her research journal.

Organizing data is facilitated by collaboration because there can be one central system that can be accessed by all collaborators. Providing a list of students (identified in an anonymous way) that reflects what data is available for each student can be a handy tool. (See Table 4.2 Data Log Sample.)

Determining the Results of the Study Because members offer diverse experiences and knowledge, they will likely offer varied insights as to the results of the study. These results will describe the data, quantitative findings, themes noted, and interpretation of what it all means to education. This part of the collaborative effort will be accomplished by sifting through the data, coding and discussing what it means, and sharing ideas. It can be helpful to view data separately at first, make notes and comments, and then meet with colleagues to share interpretations about what is evident or emerging from the data. Your group may come to a consensus or it may decide that multiple interpretations are viable based on the data, supporting theory, and related readings.

Sharing the Conclusions and Implications Here is where you would discuss how your findings or results apply to teaching and learning in the classroom. You could invite administrators to the meeting where you discuss the implications for teaching. Explain your findings and how your group thinks they apply to the curriculum and teaching.

Supporting Each Other's Ideas

We cannot stress enough that members of teacher research collaborations should be encouraged to question, comment upon, and add to colleagues' thoughts and ideas. This is how members push each other's thinking to a rich level of considering multiple options. Beebe and Masterson (2005) use the term *groupthink* to refer to an illusion that group members are all in agreement. When groups try to minimize conflict by not expressing critical thoughts in an effort to get along and work cohesively, they are guilty of groupthink (Kowert, 2002). In collaborative teacher research groups we want to avoid groupthink. Members should be encouraged to think critically and independently, evaluate comments, and insert diverse suggestions to the norm. This is done not to cause conflict but to expand and enrich the group's potential as a research team.

In some collaborative groups, one or two individuals may hold a certain perceived status or level of power or authority. For example, sometimes senior members may exert more leadership power over junior members and assume they have more to offer the group due to their experience. Sometimes, too, groups invite experts from outside their school district to help the group. It is common practice to invite college professors into a research group to be the group's connection to theory and literature. Frequently college instructors have more opportunities and resources to attend national and international conferences and do research of their own on topics in education than do K–12 teachers. Local schools can benefit from the knowledge and networking that professors are positioned to achieve. However, when new people are brought into a group, sometimes there is a perceived difference in status.

When evaluating a member's ideas, the group should not yield to perceived differences in status (Beebe & Masterson, 2005). All members should be respectful yet critical of each participant's ideas and solutions. For example, although a college professor might be knowledgeable about what current literature says about an issue and may have experience from working with other schools, he or she does not know the culture of your school, students, and teachers the way you do. Do not accept an idea or solution based solely on the status or credibility of a person; evaluate the idea on its own merits as it applies to your situation. See Appendix A, Form 7 for a helpful reproducible form to prompt discussions about Stage 3.

STAGE 4: EXPLORING THE POSSIBILITIES

Stage 4 coincides with what Tuckman (1965; Tuckman & Jensen, 1977) referred to as the Adjourning stage in which group members reflect upon, evaluate, acknowledge, or celebrate their accomplishments—or mourn their lack of productivity, if that be the case. In collaborative teacher research, however, the possibilities do not end with the culmination of the research. They extend to consider the possibilities of where the study results lead. In this section, we look at the possibilities of ongoing and final evaluation of the group's collaboration and the possibilities of continuing conversations. See Appendix A, Form 8, for a reproducible form to prompt discussion about Stage 4.

Evaluating the Group's Progress Along the Way

In collaborative groups, evaluation should be ongoing and embedded in the process and routines of the group. This can be done by devoting five minutes at the beginning of each meeting to reflect on the group's progress with the research and the group's developing relationships with each other. What should be evaluated?

- Group dynamics such as:
  - Participating: Do members actively engage in discussions and make meaningful contributions? Do they come to the group prepared to participate?
  - Listening: Do members sincerely listen to and build off of each other's ideas?
  - Respecting: Do members encourage and support the ideas of others?
  - Sharing: Do members seek out and contribute resources to the group? (Beebe & Masterson, 2005; Forsyth, 2005)
- Components specific to teacher research, such as:
  - Questioning: At all times is there an air of inquisitiveness and questioning?
  - Organizing: Are the research plan and design thoroughly thought out and are all members knowledgeable about the process? If not, what needs clarification? (Burant, Gray, Ndaw, McKinney-Keys, & Allen, 2007)
  - Ethics: Do members treat subjects and colleagues fairly, honestly, with confidentiality, and with mindful sensitivity to their needs? (Beebe & Masterson, 2005; Israel & Lassonde, 2008)
  - Recordkeeping: Is all data clearly labeled, organized, accessible to members, and securely stored?

- Evaluating: Are resources and ideas critically evaluated and discussed with members?
- Synthesizing: Are multiple perspectives considered, sorted, and brought together when appropriate through discussion? But at the same time, is there room for divergent, creative thinking?
- Applying findings: Are applications to and implications for students' learning always in the forefront of the study?

Appendix A, Form 9 offers a quick checklist that group members can reflect on during the first few minutes of each meeting. Members can set goals for the group to work toward between meetings to remedy any problem areas based on these regular, quick evaluations.

Disseminating Results and Findings

Now that you have completed your research, in what ways does the group plan to use what it has learned? How will you apply the findings to your classroom practices? Will you share them with colleagues in your school? Outside of your school? How? In what form? In what ways can your findings be used to advocate for students, for change, or for continuation of an existing program or practice?

COLLABORATION AT WORK

Practicalities of a Writing Collaboration

Contributed by Ilene Rutten and Cheryl Dozier

Our teacher research collaboration is entering its seventh year. We began working together after our teaching brought us together and we discovered that we shared many of the same beliefs and interests. We both had a deep commitment to our teaching and teacher research, we both wanted to make our teacher research results available through publication, we shared a common work ethic, we were open to suggestions, and we were celebratory people. We also both viewed writing as a generative process—that is, a process that allows us to record our thinking and come to new understandings. As we recorded our thoughts, these notes, in turn, generated additional ideas. These new ideas helped us clarify our writing, took us in a new direction, or helped us revisit our original ideas. Because the writing of teacher research is often a vulnerable space, discovering our commonalities led to a level of trust that allowed us to engage in collaborative writing.

We were intentional about the practicalities of our writing relationship. In order for us to engage in generative writing and share our teacher research, we discussed how to organize our time, our writing space, and our responsibilities. By engaging in these practices, we moved toward our goal of publication. Throughout our years together, we continued to develop our collaborative writing relationship by honoring our time commitments, our individual and joint writing responsibilities, and celebrating our accomplishments.

(continued)

(continued)

ORGANIZING OUR TIME

As we were both teaching and had family and community responsibilities, it was essential for us to block out time in our schedules for writing. We set a schedule for three to four months and then renegotiated as needed. We kept to our schedule as we both knew how easy it would be for us to cancel and attend to other matters. Once the schedule was set, and based on our previous collaborative experiences, we knew we would both be there.

WRITING SPACE

In our discussions of how to make our writing collaboration successful, we discussed how to organize our writing space. Cheryl offered her workspace. This was a considerable commitment on her part. Cheryl was willing to share her personal space and make room for research data, numerous drafts, and idea folders. We quickly discovered that sitting side by side was the most productive arrangement for us. This allowed us to simultaneously view the data, previous drafts, and our current document on the computer screen.

NEGOTIATED RESPONSIBILITIES

Though we worked in Cheryl's workspace on Cheryl's computer, we took turns writing. Most often Cheryl would begin the process and then after an hour or so would ask that I take over. I would write for awhile and then suggest that Cheryl take over. We always exchanged places when asked, as we respected each other's requests. At times, the person at the computer ran out of ideas, at other times one of us was more familiar with the material and it was easier for her to do the writing. We would exchange three or four times during each writing session. For us, the process of changing writers helped us be more productive, as the intensity of writing, though exciting, can often be depleting. At the end of each writing session, we always created an agenda for our next meeting. The agenda helped us quickly move into the next session's writing as we had recorded what needed to happen next. These agendas often took the format of a sticky note attached to Cheryl's computer or a bolded note at the bottom of the manuscript. At times, we had numerous items to attend to so we would prioritize the list. Often we would attach names to the items on the agenda, especially if they needed to be completed during times we were not together.

GENERATIVE PROCESS

As we began to write each new segment for our manuscript, we would discuss what message we wanted to convey. After developing a focus, whoever was sitting at the computer would capture our "first-draft thinking." Our first-draft thinking took many forms. At times we made lists or notes, at other times we wrote in narrative form. As we began to flesh out our focus on the computer, we offered additional suggestions and ideas to what we were reading on the screen. This first-draft writing captured as many ideas as possible, knowing we would revisit our draft numerous times. At other times, we decided during our agenda preparation to write segment drafts on our own. We volunteered to do one of the segments, we decided by level of expertise, or we just divided up the workload. These segments became a starting point for our writing the next time we met.

LONG-DISTANCE COLLABORATIVE WRITING

Three years ago Ilene moved halfway across the country and began a new job. We have now established a long-distance writing collaboration. We set phone appointments and talk for approximately an hour about our manuscript. The frequency of our appointments depends on the project in which we're currently involved and the deadlines we have set for ourselves (or that others have set for us). Sometimes we talk every day; other times we may need time to write in between appointments, so we talk less regularly. As we did with our in-person writing, we set an agenda for each phone appointment. At times we decided, during our agenda preparation, to reread certain sections to review our transitions. Or we agreed to prepare new segments to insert into the manuscript before our next phone conversation. If we inserted a segment that we had not previously discussed, we highlighted this new text in blue to remind us to review that particular piece. During our phone conversations we both have the manuscript in front of us on our screens. Using our notes, we discuss revisions and enter them as we talk.

For us, negotiating the practicalities of our writing collaboration made our time together productive and rewarding. By discussing how to organize our time, our writing space, and our responsibilities, we used our time efficiently, which moved us toward our goal of publication. Our writing collaboration was initially successful and continues to be successful because we share common interests and beliefs and we trust the commitments we have made to one another in our teacher research collaboration.

Reflecting On and Evaluating the Work

In the final stage of the collaborative teacher research group's work, the group takes a final look at what has been accomplished, productive and unproductive behaviors of the group, and how they would improve the process for the next time. This is a time of celebration and recognition of each other's contributions. Though evaluation has been ongoing throughout the process, in Stage 4, sharing final reflections will bring closure to the group's work. See Exhibit 5.1 and its reproducible version in Appendix A, Form 10, for a final reflections activity, which includes thoughts for planning next steps.

EXHIBIT 5.1: FINAL REFLECTIONS

Discuss the following questions with your group:

1. What have we accomplished in our collaboration? How does this relate to our mission statement?

(continued)

(*continued*)

2. What group behaviors, procedures, and contributions were productive? How could we improve them?
   What group behaviors, procedures, and contributions were unproductive? How would we change them next time?
   Will the group work together again? In what capacity? What will it study?

STAGE 5: ONGOING CONVERSATIONS

Now that a synergy has been created among your group of participants, you will most likely find that once the study is over and the findings have been shared, members of the group continue to respond to each other in certain situations in this research persona. You will seek each other out when circumstances arise in which you want to talk with someone about something you have observed in your classroom or an article you recently came across in a professional journal. The members of your group came together because they had a common interest or concern. That interest remains a thread among group members.

When you reach this stage, you know you have truly developed a collaborative community or a system. Knowing you have each other to talk with and rely on, even after the study, will increase what you as a reflective practitioner are able to offer your students (Garmston & Wellman, 2008). In this stage, ask yourself these questions:

- What can I continue to offer to my colleagues so we can develop deeper understandings of how our study's findings apply to students?

- How can I continue to learn from the expertise of my colleagues?

See Appendix A, Form 11, for a reproducible form to prompt discussion about Stage 5.

Melding Voices Through Collaboration

In talking about the collaboration process they experienced together, one of the groups that Cindy works with discovered that their relationship had developed so deeply that their voices in the project began to meld together. Furthermore, what they learned about collaborating during the project actually could be applied to the expectations they held for their students' collaborative group work. Read about their idea of the Invisible Researcher and how this concept applies to students' learning in this chapter's Effective Implementation feature.

THINKING TOGETHER: THE BIRTH OF THE INVISIBLE RESEARCHER

Contributed by Carolyn Chryst, Zanna McKay, and Cindy Lassonde

We are a group of elementary education teacher educators. We formed a collaborative teacher research group to reflect on our teaching practices. At one of our collaborative meetings, we just naturally started to share our thoughts about teaching and learning. This sharing led us into intense conversations about how our collaboration reflected and shaped our development as teacher researchers, instructors, and academic writers.

We discovered that through the collaboration process we were each adopting the best of each other. Along the way, a fourth voice was developing among us. One day, while writing together, Carolyn said, "This idea is brilliant. Which one of you wrote it?" None of us could identify the specific author! Our individual voices and writing styles had melded into a powerful fourth voice. We began to call this the voice of the Invisible Researcher.

The results of our research, if expressed by any one of us or even just two of us, would not resonate with the same voice or possibly not even encompass the same results. The old adage "The whole is greater than the sum of its parts" is manifest in this collaboration. When all the individual and overlapping parts are added together, energy is created, creativity is restored, and the will to keep marching is revived. As the collaboration takes on more and more elements of community, it becomes stronger, more powerful, and efficient. Thoughts about this Invisible Researcher led to thinking about how the idea applies to our expectations and hopes for our students' collaborative work.

When we ask our students to do group work—to collaborate—we often get individuals presenting parts. We try to get them to rise above their individual talents to become more than any one of them could have accomplished in the same time frame on their own. As instructors preparing future teachers for a workforce that demands ever more collaborative and committee work, we need to help establish the skills and mindset needed to be successful. We have learned from our research that:

1. The combination of individuals is not as important as helping them capitalize on each other's strengths. This melding is how the fourth voice, a synthesis of all voices, develops.

2. Although the goal is to meld voices, it is still important to recognize and value each individual's strengths and contributions to the project. No egos are allowed! For example, one may do all the background research, while another types and keeps records; both contributions are critical to the success of the project.

3. A collective plan of action with deadlines needs to be established and agreed on at the close of each meeting. This avoids the tragedy of the commons where no one takes responsibility by assuming that others have. A clear plan of action with assigned tasks reduces opportunities of one group member taking over, causing others to feel resentful and offer less and less input.

4. Members need individual tasks as well as overlapping tasks with at least one other member to keep the project moving toward a collective ownership of the project. Though it may feel inefficient, the combination of results is always better than the individual parts.

5. A sense of "our work" versus "my work" has to be established to open the process to creativity and deeper insights. It is in the overlapping of the parts and the building of group ownership that the invisible researcher comes to the party and helps to deepen each individual's perspective and understanding. This, in turn, adds to the collective, which deepens understanding, which adds to the collective . . . You get the picture.

BEYOND THE STAGES

Now that you are aware of all of the stages of dynamic group dynamics as they apply to learning communities and teacher research, there is much more to discover. In Chapter Six you will learn about collaborating effectively in ethical ways.

PART

3

Collaborating Effectively

INTRODUCTION

MIDDLE GROUNDS
By Cindy Lassonde

If I value you and you value me
We meet in the middle
And try to agree.

We don't turn our backs
And ignore who we are.
We don't close our minds
And glare from afar.

We listen, consider,
Adjust, and align.
We chitter and chatter
Until we are fine.

If I value you and you value me
We meet in the middle
And try to agree.

Our values have a lot to do with how we perceive and respond to others. We are more likely to put forth time and effort when we value something or someone than when we do not. In this part-opening poem, the author considers the role of communication in a relationship and how our determination of how much we value a relationship can influence our work with others.

Part Three opens with a discussion about the ethical considerations that will help improve collaboration and group dynamics, then continues on with a chapter on leadership strategies. As you read these chapters, reflect on how lines in "Middle Grounds" connect to the ideas in these chapters. Think about how much influence considerate or inconsiderate communication (or a lack of communication) can have on our collaborative work and our positions as leaders. Also, the Reflection Questions and Study Group Exercises found in Appendixes B and C will help all readers focus on the main points of the chapters.

6

Ethical Considerations
Improving Group Dynamics

How to Use This Chapter

- When teacher study groups or other professional learning communities engage in collaborative research projects, ethical issues can occasionally arise. The purpose of this chapter is to offer a foundation for considering the role of ethics in pursuing collaborative research activities and also to provide background definitions and information along with scenarios and suggested strategies for improving group dynamics. The chapter will help you to address the following questions:

    - What actions does our group need to take to function effectively and efficiently as well as ethically?

    - How do the goals of our group influence effective strategies we want to support in order to deal with ethical dilemmas that arise?

    - How can the guidelines we establish be used to avoid and to effectively cope with behavioral issues of group members from an ethical perspective?

    - What is our understanding of what it means to be ethical when participating in a collaborative group?

  Having a set of ethical standards or guidelines can support group functioning by allowing you to consider to the extent to which group members treat subjects and colleagues fairly, honestly, with confidentiality, and with mindful sensitivity to their needs (Beebe & Masterson, 2005; Israel & Lassonde, 2007). In addition, such guidelines can help measure the actions of the group and ensure that ethics are maintained (Israel & Lassonde, 2007). This chapter will present an overview of ethical considerations to help you develop an awareness of the role of ethics in group functioning, behavior, and overall decision making. It will provide a rationale to help you establish ethical practices within your collaborative group and will include examples and case studies, as well as several personal stories from the authors to help inform your thinking. At the end of the chapter we offer ten essential steps for establishing effective ethical guidelines for managing successful collaborations. Let's begin our discussion about ethics and collaborative groups!

WHAT IS ETHICAL COLLABORATION?

What is ethics and how does it connect to collaborative teacher research? The field of ethics has to do with what is good and bad and what is perceived as one's moral duty, values, and obligations (Israel & Lassonde, 2007). As you read in the second verse of the opening poem in Part One, *An N* of One No More* by C. F. Chryst, "Some nodded; some smiled; some derided." Essentially, groups are held together by common pursuit of shared learning experiences. Shared learning experiences also include the pathway to one's moral duty. As stated in Chapter One, "By engaging in meaningful practices, they become involved in discussions and actions that make a difference to the communities they value."

When Zeichner (2003) refers to building community through rituals and routines, ethics guides this construction by framing the expectations determined by group members. Therefore, ethical collaboration revolves around group consensus of what it means to act ethically within and outside of the collaboration. As Garmston and Wellman (1999) state, "It is our values that drive our goal clarity about who we are, how we want to be together, and what we will accomplish for students" (p. 31).

The ethical standards that form a group's foundation and offer a guiding light for how to work together can be framed around your mission. These standards may be derived from the ethical standards that guide professional groups most relevant to your work, from the ethical standards issued by your school, university, or other supporting institutions, or from other groups of stakeholders who are involved. As a first step, we recommend that you obtain and review the ethical guidelines set forth by a professional educational organization in which you may be involved. For example, because the authors of this book are members of the International Reading Association (IRA), we would first begin a review of the ethical standards set forth by this association, which are briefly summarized in Exhibit 6.1. A detailed review can be easily obtained at the IRA Web site www.reading.org.

Exhibit 6.1: Summary of Ethical Standards for the International Reading Association

CURRICULUM AND INSTRUCTION

It is the ethical responsibility of all IRA members to use curriculum materials and instructional methods that:

- Are consistent with IRA position statements.
- Are based on evidence.

- Differentiate instruction to meet the individual needs of all students.
- Are free from cultural and linguistic bias.
- Represent multiple perspectives and interpretations.
- Are based on valid and reliable print and technological sources of information.

ASSESSING, DIAGNOSING, AND EVALUATING

It is the ethical responsibility of all IRA members to assess, diagnose, and evaluate student growth using instruments that:

- Are valid and reliable.
- Are free from cultural and linguistic bias.
- Are consistent with IRA position statements.
- Are administered in accordance with instrument specifications.
- Are interpreted in a manner consistent with the instruments' purpose.
- Are used in ways that protect the confidentiality of students and families.

CREATING A LITERATE ENVIRONMENT

It is the ethical responsibility of all IRA members to create literate environments that:

- Include all students.
- Are free from bias.
- Encourage collaboration.
- Provide equitable access to books, technology-based information, and nonprint materials representing multiple levels, broad interests, and diverse cultural and linguistic backgrounds.
- Are consistent with IRA position statements.
- Are responsive to student interests, reading abilities, and backgrounds.
- Are structured to help students learn to work cooperatively and productively with others.

EXEMPLIFYING PROFESSIONALISM

It is the ethical responsibility of all IRA members to exhibit professionalism by:

- Honestly representing oneself and one's work.
- Maintaining professional relationships.
- Demonstrating positive dispositions toward reading and the teaching of reading.
- Actively working to advance IRA positions, policies, and practices.
- Conducting research that is:
  - Honest.

(*continued*)

(continued)

- Respectful of human dignity.
- Respectful of peer input.
- Grounded in a strong theoretical and research base.
- Free from bias.
- A significant contribution to understanding the reading process and the teaching of reading.
- Publishing research that is:
  - Original, and does not plagiarize previously published research.
  - Honestly represented.
  - Valid and reliable.
  - Respectful of previously published research.

Source: Code of Ethics—IRA's Code of Ethics, Conflict of Interest Policy, Describing Professional Conduct (March, 2008). International Reading Association.

Once you obtain the guidelines established by a relevant professional organization, we suggest that you review them and discuss them with your collaborative group. As you can see, the Code of Ethics for our association is very specific and focuses on four key areas: Curriculum and Instruction; Assessing, Diagnosing, and Evaluating; Creating a Literate Environment; and Exemplifying Professionalism. These key areas help guide us in conversations related to ethical standards.

As we hope you realized in reading the preceding chapters, a goal of collaborative research communities is to offer safe places for colleagues to explore, learn, and bond—as professionals and personally. It is through the process of collaboration that what you value the most will emerge and be tested. Ethical values become the vehicle to help guide your thinking about the principled ways in which you will act. In other words, how you nod, how you smile, and whether or not you decide to deride.

A BRIEF STORY ABOUT ETHICS AND PERCEIVED VALUES

When Cindy was working with Karen and Krislynn on their collaborative study of Book Clubs Plus, they shared details about what was happening in their classrooms and students' work. It became apparent that Cindy and Karen had different expectations for their students that revolved around each instructor's perceived value for accountability. Whereas Cindy required students to keep written logs of their readings and reflections, Karen relied on observation of class discussions to assess students' progress. This sparked conversations about teaching styles, processes, and outcomes. What kinds of ethical considerations might these types of conversations potentially rouse in a collaborative research project? How do we develop collaborations that respect and even grow from our differences in philosophy in moral and ethical ways?

Ethical Collaborations to Consider

Collaborative groups will engage in a variety of research endeavors. From an ethical perspective it is important to follow research practices that are guided by ethical and moral decision making. For example, in one collaborative group a member enjoys the writing aspect but finds difficulty with online collaborations:

> Jane enjoys working in collaborative groups. She especially likes to work on the writing aspect of research projects. One of her responsibilities is as editor of the manuscripts. She frequently makes content changes to the manuscripts, in addition to the editorial responsibilities. What Jane doesn't do is include new references to the new or revised contents. Her team (or group) members are not happy and have requested Jane use track changes when editing. They would also appreciate it if Jane would ask permission before making major changes. If you were a member of this group how would you handle this situation? Do you prefer to talk openly in your group and confront issues? Does your group prefer to ignore the problem and accept the changes without references?

With the use of technology integrated in collaborative groups, ethics plays an important role in how the group documents or uses information. Online groups working together through technology face ethical decisions when trying to make sense of how to interpret and communicate online discourse in a way that is positive and nonthreatening. Our experiences with online collaboratives have been positive in that we have been fortunate to work with colleagues who, rather than infer and misinterpret the intent of the text, will inquire for clarification before making a judgment about the interpretation.

We think what is important to keep in mind when working in online collaboratives is that as professionals we still need to adhere to high standards by creating technology environments that are healthy and positive while keeping the main mission of the research project in the forefront. Sometimes e-mails can be interpreted in the wrong way. This happens because the writer's voice in e-mail is lost and needs to be substituted by the reader. The reader and the writer may not have the same understanding, which creates dissonance. Avoiding this type of unhealthy environment when associated with online collaboratives can be discussed when the group is getting established and prior to major decision-making steps.

When Conflict Arises

In gathering material for this book, the authors were amazed by the number of collaborative communities that exist and are going strong across the world. The concept is growing in leaps and bounds. To gather information, we distributed a survey (see Appendix E) to various teacher groups and professional listservs, such as the International Reading Association (IRA) Teacher as Researcher Subcommittee, the Ethics Subcommittee, the Teaching as a Researching Profession Special Interest Group, the American Educational Research Association's (AERA) Action Research Special Interest Group, the International Teacher Research Network, and the National Reading Council.

As you recall, the authors of this book conducted an online search for collaborative groups and found a number of Web sites dedicated to supporting these learning communities. We approached these groups to complete our survey, too. Some of the responses addressed ethical issues. We learned that the groups that did function ethically took steps to prevent issues that could turn divisive to the group at a later point. Their recommendations included:

- One or two people who the group feels have a reputation for being fair mediators should be identified as conflict resolvers.

- Members who feel uncomfortable with another member should go to the resolvers for help.

- Issues that arise should be discussed at the next meeting or privately among those concerned as appropriate. The resolvers should treat the matter tactfully, honestly, and ethically.

Now that you have an overview of a few ways ethics can play a role in how a collaborative group functions successfully, think about the following questions. Has your group discussed guidelines for conducting research, meeting collaboratively, and how information will be communicated during the research process? If not, or if those guidelines need to be revisited, now would be a good time to write that down as a discussion item and place it on the agenda for the next meeting.

Read the following Collaboration at Work feature to help you begin to think more deeply about the role of ethics in collaborative groups. Doing right and working in an ethical manner enabled Rebecca Rogers and Mary Ann Kramer to form a group that looked at social justice issues effectively. The group was able to work well together because ethical standards guided their work. Before reading this case example, think about the following questions: What is it the group is doing right that enables them to work effectively and avoid ethical issues? What standards would you say guide the group's overall mission and work?

COLLABORATION AT WORK

The Literacy for Social Justice Teacher Research Group in St. Louis, Missouri
Contributed by Rebecca Rogers and Mary Ann Kramer

The Literacy for Social Justice Teacher Research Group is a grassroots, teacher-led professional development group located in St. Louis, Missouri. It is committed to literacy education and advocacy as it relates to social justice in classrooms and communities. Founded in 2001 by Rebecca Rogers and Mary Ann Kramer, our group rotates between teacher-inquiry projects, teacher-led professional development, and actions and advocacy as they relate to literacy education.

What was helpful in setting up the group? It seems like we are continually "setting up" the group—even after seven years of existence. Our people, focus, structure, and agenda constantly change to be responsive to the local context. We think this is one of the reasons the group continues to grow and evolve. Other variables supporting our longevity and effectiveness include the following:

a. Having two organizers who have different networks of people and hold expertise in literacy education and social justice across the lifespan.

b. Sharing responsibilities between the organizers and other members of the group. We have a "core leadership team" that consists of six to eight people. The leadership team makes decisions about our programs and goals throughout the year. We generally have fifteen people at each of our workshops (held twice a month). Our base consists of over two hundred people who are on our listserv and attend our annual events and actions (such as rallies and our annual Educating for Change Curriculum Fair).

c. Focusing on a participatory design; meeting the needs of the group as the members changed and evolved.

d. Accessing university resources—journals, meeting spaces, and eventually funding and Web space for our Web site and listserv.

e. Offering various "perks" to people in the group was important—opportunities to present at conferences; books and professional development resources; opportunities to write articles and chapters; workshops on activism and advocacy.

f. Bringing together folks who traditionally did not get together: K–12 educators, university people, community activists, and adult literacy education teachers. Where we met was often a topic of discussion for us. Some people in the group thought meeting at the university was good for people who were generally not on the university campus, because it opened up a new set of resources for them. Others felt that meeting in the community signaled that university people were willing to move beyond the university campus. Often, we rotated between the two sites, often for pragmatic reasons. For the past two years, we have met only at the adult learning site, located in the city of St. Louis.

g. Connecting with Rethinking Schools and a national coalition of teacher activists called TAG (Teacher Activist Group) was important to our group. TAG consists of teacher activist groups in New York (Collective of Radical Educators), Chicago (Teachers for Social Justice), and San Francisco (Teachers 4 Social Justice). Being in this national coalition helps us to make ongoing connections between local, national, and international contexts. We share strategies for organizing, recruiting, and developing leadership within our groups. We also serve as allies and plan similar actions in our cities. The Teachers for Social Justice group in Chicago inspired us to start an annual curriculum fair that showcases teachers presenting curriculum that is based in social justice principles.

More information about the Literacy for Social Justice Teacher Research Group can be found at www.umsl.edu/~lsjtrg/.

INVESTING IN DIALOGUE

As you read in the preceding case study, the role of ethics was key to the successful collaboration. What the group did well was to use dialogue as a tool to promote ideas and thinking about social justice, as well as ideas about the organizational and behavioral structures of the group. For example, they used dialogue to guide how they would dispense the responsibilities of the group. Dialogue promoted a way to honor members' voices, as well as to benefit from individual strengths that help in making collaboration a success. Respect for peer input was shown through engaging in conversations and encouraging individualism. In addition, the tasks were rotated among the group members so that no one member felt overwhelmed. This also provided a window into how group members' strengths became valued.

In summary, groups should invest in a dialogue about how they will demonstrate that they value the voices of the group's members, what measures they will take to ensure that the intellectual property of the group follows ethical standards, how they will act in a manner that indicates they value working relationships of members, and how they will create platforms that allow group members to be adequately acknowledged.

You have been given insight about the role of ethics up until this point. Think back to the original questions asked at the beginning of this chapter. Using your new knowledge about the role of ethics and the guidelines you propose for your group, use the following Thinking Together feature story to see if the guidelines established will be effective.

THINKING TOGETHER: ETHICAL COLLABORATION

Mary was very involved in the collaboration when it was initiated. She was one of the forming members who helped shape the research questions, write the mission statement, and invite members to join the collaboration. However, as the school year wore on and her schedule became more and more demanding, she neglected several commitments that she originally made to the group. To compensate, others had to fulfill her obligations as well as their own. Along with these neglected obligations that others took over, Mary seldom came to group meetings and made excuses about not having the time to write regularly in her research journal.

There are two issues to consider here: the group's ethical approach to managing the problem and Mary's ethical commitment. How would your group approach a member like Mary who is not living up to the expectations of the collaborative group? Under what circumstances do Mary as well as all other group members have an ethical obligation to support the group once they have committed to the collaboration?

BEHAVIORAL ISSUES AND THE ROLE OF ETHICS

The behavior or personality characteristics are related to the actions of group members and interactions within the group as a whole. It is important that all members know each other, and an understanding of differences within the community needs to be established before collaboration occurs. Like any relationship, effective communication is based on trust. Maintaining members' positive attitude is important to the overall success of the group. Behavioral strengths that define a group are related to the following elements:

1. Collegiality of group members
2. Ability of members to support one another in a constructive manner

3. Respecting diversity and individuality with the group
4. Willingness to share ideas and to think critically about issues
5. Demonstrating enthusiasm related to topics of inquiry and research

Some reflective questions that focus on behavioral characteristics of group members follow:

1. When problems arise, how will group members treat each other?
2. Do group members see stumbling blocks as obstacles but turn them into positives?
3. Do group members remain flexible in thinking and decision making, while remaining tolerant and appreciative of differences?
4. Can vigorous interactions develop a deeper understanding and appreciation for each other?
5. What unique behavioral characteristics can I bring to the group that will allow me to have a successful experience?
6. Do group members talk openly and with respect for others, while being able to confront issues right away?
7. Does the group frequently evaluate individual roles and each member's personal level of collegiality with others?
8. What does it mean to act in a collegial manner within a group?
9. What ethical dilemmas do you foresee might occur in your group?
10. How might your group avoid them?
11. What problem-solving tactics would you employ if such ethical dilemmas do occur?

Some factors that might contribute to negative behaviors typically are related to failing to demonstrate a basic level of respect for group members. For example, some of the following actions were reported to contribute to a negative attitude within a group:

- Informal meetings cause a feeling of being left out
- Individual concerns about working collaboratively with others
- Resistance to change
- Not feeling comfortable with open conflict and dialogue
- Disagreeing in a loud manner with group members, or being confrontational
- Personal health issues

Working in collaborative groups is not always easy for everyone. Some people tend to thrive in groups whereas others exhibit behavioral characteristics that are not conducive to effective group participation. Recognizing group members' strengths and weaknesses early on and discussing how behavioral factors will be handled will limit any potential setbacks caused by unexpected actions of others.

Certain other factors that contribute to behavioral issues can also be related to research and not necessarily due to personality conflicts. For example, one collaborative research group believes the effectiveness of the research and the group is primarily related to the selection of the research topic.

When projects are individual and depend on the person's interests and setting, then personal interest influences the group projects. This is an important insight when considering research. The statement implies that when research is imposed on a group or a member, behavioral motivation might decrease.

ESTABLISHING EFFECTIVE ETHICAL GUIDELINES

Proceeding in collaborative groups without an established set of ethical guidelines is not recommended by the authors of this book. In fact, we speak from personal experience. We ourselves did not always agree on procedures during this book's development. In coming together we were ultimately guided by what we believed was best for the book, including the content and the needs of the audience. The resolutions were related to the ability of the group, the authors, and the editor, to change. Change in values is not always easy. As Garmston and Wellman (1999) propose, values help determine who we are, our work with students, and our interactions with others. The following points can be used to establish the ethical guidelines within your group. The discussion is arranged in a format summarized in Table 6.1 for you to use with your group and to create a set of your own action steps. The ten steps discussed in the table will help extract certain ideas related to what group members value, as well as how to use values to guide the role of ethics within the group. This type of structure supports the IRA beliefs mentioned above, as well.

TABLE 6.1. *Ten Steps to Create Ethical Guidelines and Action Steps in Collaborative Groups*

Values	Key Discussion Points	Action Steps the Group Will Take
1. In reviewing the ethical standards of the organization of importance, we believe . . .		
2. Ethics means . . .		
3. The way we want our group to function is . . .		
4. When problems arise with group members we . . .		
5. We will communicate during group discussions and during online discussions in a manner that is . . .		
6. Each group member values . . .		
7. We have discussed the key elements of what ethics means and we . . .		
8. When we face problems with the behavior of a group member we will . . .		
9. We have investigated the specific ethical practices that our research follows, such as working with students, or parents, and we . . .		
10. We have created a conflict resolution plan that is democratic, justifiable, and equitable.		

THE BENEFITS

You have learned in this chapter that ethics plays a key role in the function and form of collaborative groups. In order to maintain a safe place for colleagues to explore, learn, and bond both professionally and personally, groups can establish ethical guidelines to follow. Such guidelines can be used to avoid or solve problems. In the next chapter you will use the information gained in this chapter to help establish the leadership role with a collaborative group. Let's proceed!

Leadership Strategies for Collaborative Support Groups

How to Use This Chapter

This chapter discusses leadership roles and effective organizational and managerial strategies within collaborative settings regardless of the collaborative model. Previously, Chapter Four outlined how a teacher leader or administrator integrates collaborative teacher research as a means of job-embedded, teacher-led professional development for faculty or groups. You discovered specific ideas and suggestions for the formation and organization of collaborative groups. Content, case studies, and research provided you with foundational knowledge in the developmental stages for a collaborative study to form and function. Specific strategies provided insight into why school leaders and coaches should or should not participate in such groups and the type of issues resulting from such participation.

This chapter will help leaders of such collaborative groups utilize this prior knowledge and individual leadership experience to gain a better understanding of how to lead effectively within collaborative group models. One of the specific questions addressed in this chapter is: What role should school leaders have in such groups? Contributor quotes from the Fairfax school district are included as references for support to leaders who want authentic models.

INTRODUCTION

Both authors of this book have been involved with collaborative research groups, some of which were quite effective. However, we were also involved with other groups that were not so effective. Both types of experiences were valuable when writing and reflecting on the ingredients for successful collaborative groups.

This chapter provides effective leadership strategies for collaborative groups. In addition, this chapter will look at some of the more frequent challenges that leaders of collaborative research groups might face, along with strategies that work and do not work when facing these challenges.

If you are a leader of a group or organization working collaboratively, or the person in charge of starting a new research group, this information is useful when getting established in a leadership role. If you are in existing collaborative groups, this chapter will help you improve effectiveness. Teachers and researchers can use this information when making decisions about joining collaborative groups or evaluating their behaviors within such a group. Administrators can also benefit from this information when establishing policies for teacher research, professional development, and collaborative groups. This chapter will discuss each of the three key components faced in leadership roles within collaborative groups. They are:

- Organizational Strategies
- Motivational Strategies
- Professional Strategies

TAKING A CLOSE LOOK AT LEADERSHIP SUCCESS STRATEGIES

Organizational Strategies

The organizational structure is related to how the group operates, the basic guidelines that have been established, how the group communicates, and the overall pragmatics established by the group. Prior to or during the first meeting, the group will need to start thinking about certain decisions regarding the desired organizational structure. The following checklist can be used as an agenda or a guide when having such a discussion.

1. What is our overall goal of the leader and group?
2. Do we want to establish our mission?
3. When should we hold our meetings?
4. How much time will be given for discussion, or for sharing new ideas?
5. Do we have established roles for each group member?
6. Have we invited others familiar with our line of inquiry?
7. Have we made decisions about how to monitor commitments of group members?
8. Will we use time during meetings to strategize and get tasks done?
9. Will we rotate leadership, circulate papers by e-mail, or post documents to a Web board?
10. Will we encourage growth with new members?

As you can see, there are many things to consider as a leader. This list is not exhaustive, but by making organizational decisions early on less time will be spent on issues that might arise later. Making decisions about the organization of the group prior to beginning a group will enhance overall effectiveness and success. If groups are not well organized in advance, organization becomes the greatest challenge and hindrance to the success of the group, resulting in less time being spent on the groups' collaborative task or project goals.

If organizational decisions are not made early on by leaders, chaos occurs, resulting in insignificant issues dragging down the group. Several issues that will have a negative impact on the organizational structure include the following:

Issues with Time Management   Following are situations that may arise:

- Difficulty scheduling meeting times that work for everyone, and just finding the time to meet regularly.
- Spending too much time on organizational issues and not leaving enough time for research updates.
- Coordinating schedules and school calendars.
- The size of the group—be it too large—might make writing a challenge because there are too many voices in the work. Or, too many members may make some members feel disengaged due to lack of participation. Too small of a group, on the other hand, may limit the depth of discussion, knowledge, and perceptions offered.

Issues with Group Members   These issues might come up:

- Team members become dispersed because of job relocation or personal matters.
- Fluctuation of membership causes a constant review of the research, mission, and goals, leading to a lack of progress in the research agenda.
- Uninformed individuals who are not involved with the research, such as principals or reading coaches substituting for another member, wind up running meetings.
- A mix of people with a vision for the big picture or small details may cause some members to be frustrated and may stall the progress of the project.
- Members haven't established in advance ways to work together effectively, causing discord and disorganization that must be managed and restructured in the midst of the project.
- Members' individual goals might conflict with the group's research goals or the school's goals for the group.

Issues with Recordkeeping   The following items are vital to consider:

- New group tasks that emerge over time such as assessments, report writing, and analysis
- Lack of organization when new ideas are being introduced
- Updating Web sites and storing information electronically for future reference
- Confidentiality of inquiry, as well as adherence to copyright issues or internal review boards
- Preparation of presentation materials and assessment tools related to measuring effectiveness

In summary, establishing a clear organizational structure prior to beginning a collaborative research project is extremely important for the group's leader. As one respondent notes,

We documented baseline results in their own testing regimens, and then met for two years, once per week for periods of 1–3 hours, to review and compare results of general testing and teaching, identify overlaps in perceived difficulties, share knowledge of their disciplines as it related to students' general language and literacy achievement, determine additional strategy work in other areas of development, and to suggest and implement general supportive lessons in resource rooms and classrooms.

Convenience was more important for another collaborative research group that found meeting regularly during school hours was more effective.

We met regularly as a group in formal meetings, which evolved from weekly meetings in 2003–2004 to regular monthly program meetings which are ongoing. We also met informally around the lunch table and continued discussions. However, not all faculties engage in this lunch table sharing.

—Ann Taylor, Southern Illinois University Edwardsville

Motivational Strategies

Motivational factors are related to the psychological portion that increases or decreases a group's productivity. Intrinsic and extrinsic motivators play a role in a collaborative group similar to the way in which motivators affect student performance in the classroom. Generally, in order to be engaged one needs to have a motivation. Some questions that can be considered by the leaders and presented to the group during early meetings are as follows:

1. What is the driving force behind the group?
2. Does professional gain influence motivation for involvement?
3. Is sharing research findings with other peers important?
4. Is a desire to be acknowledged for the work of the group a driving force guiding the research?
5. Are teaching reform and implementing collaborative goals within the community valued?
6. Does the goal of student achievement play a role in the progress of the group?
7. Is student learning a focus at all times?
8. How important is freedom of choice when working on research?

Certain factors minimize motivation to continue working on research and being a member within a collaborative group. The factors listed below stem from issues that were not discussed when organizing the group, or were caused by degrees of difficulty related to the research being conducted. These factors include:

- No time to conduct research can cause frustrations or too many breaks in the research
- Intensity of the research work creates struggles and conflicts
- Experienced teachers who do not value research have difficulty buying into the overall process or goals of the group
- Budget and funding or a lack of financial support
- Publication, or presentation opportunities are not available due to financial constraints
- Recognition that project is valuable
- Passion for content of study
- Publishing and networking ability
- Longevity of group and ability to maintain a variety of voices and experiences
- Power or control issues that may arise based on the financial backing of a project and the expectations or agenda of those providing the funding

Although not all groups are motivated by the same factors, it is important for leaders to be aware of what types of issues or actions can help with motivation or hinder progress. One group, realizing the value of building in time to value small successes that occur as the research progresses, writes the following:

Each summer we have had a summer institute which gives the group a chance to recharge and reflect on the past year and plan for the future year. This was an important sustaining structure for us as a group. One year we held a literacy and power institute and invited national speakers to come speak with us. . . .Yet another year we held sessions where we strategized where the group had been, where it was, and where it was going.

Professional Strategies

Technical supports are related to the expertise that group members have to offer, access to resources such as research, technology, and administrative assistance. Questions for the group to consider when thinking deeply about the technical resources available are as follows:

1. Have we discussed technical areas of expertise and personal networking connections?
2. Do we need to identify where we will obtain specific necessary resources, or whom to contact to obtain the knowledge?
3. Have we sorted out what we already know about a specific area and what gaps of knowledge might exist?
4. Will we need to establish links with larger literacy groups in our area or in the country who might assist us in our research?
5. Have we made a list of the available personal and technical resources?
6. Do we need to learn about institutional issues and policies in advance that might affect the research and effectiveness of the group?
7. Do we lack knowledge in specific areas and should we consider inviting specialists as guests to our group?
8. Do group members have a solid understanding of what collaboration means within the group?
9. Are we able to effectively communicate collaborative conceptual process with teachers indirectly involved in research?

One of the biggest challenges for leaders of collaborative groups seems to be the level of technical supports; therefore, expertise in a specific area is important to the success of the group or the ability to know where to find the knowledge that is lacking. In addition, groups tend to give attention to the methodology that suits their research agenda in favor of more general issues of tasks and learning. Other areas that affect the technical ability that causes problems for the group are:

*   Not understanding publicists' venue requirements for publishing
*   Different views on policies and practices that influence decision making of the group
*   Not being aware of Internal Review Board procedures
*   Lack of understanding related to strategies for conducting research in a classroom
*   Unaware of copyright laws and other related legal matters
*   Having to conduct research outside one's area of expertise without proper training or knowledge-building efforts on the topic

One group responds to technical issue of providing a global focus of the group as follows: "AR Expeditions was created as an online peer-reviewed journal to provide a venue through which action researchers might share their work or ideas. This journal and our SIG newsletter serve to get information out and provide a venue through which we can share information, ideas, results, or resources with each other." (See AR Expeditions at www.arexpeditions.montana.edu/index.php.)

COLLABORATION AT WORK

The Action Research Collaborative
Contributed by Jane Zeni

For sixteen years, members of the Action Research Collaborative (ARC) have met monthly to share works in progress. Most of us teach at area universities; some are school-based teacher research team leaders. We see the meetings as a way to keep ourselves honest—to learn and talk and write about our own practice rather than to settle for being the outside experts guiding other people's research.

The success of our group is related, I think, to its minimal structure:

- ARC is a voluntary group, independent from control by any university, school district, or funding agency. Members neither pay nor get paid to attend.
- There is rotating leadership (members to chair the meetings, schedule each month's presenter, reserve the meeting room, and keep the coffeepot). No single person is the force behind ARC.
- The structure is self-sustaining, with no cost for circulating papers by e-mail. The presenter brings the bagels, so there is also no need for a refreshment kitty.

Simple ground rules spare us from the boring summaries typical of academic conferences. Each member is expected to have read the paper (at least skimmed it) before the meeting. The presenter has just a short while to introduce the work (if a presenter talks more than five minutes, somebody is bound to break in with a question).

The ARC tradition has led to highly stimulating, nonstuffy meetings. The free-floating discussion usually takes off from a paper in several directions, with expert feedback punctuated by laughter and offbeat suggestions. This can be scary for a new researcher (but we tend to move lightly with grad students). At the same time, ARC has been enormously helpful to young faculty working for tenure and for experienced researchers with a book in progress. The diversity of membership jogs our thinking in ways that are not limited to, "you need a transition here" or "check the reference there."

Members are welcome to bring work to the group at any stage in development. One month's presenter may share samples of field notes and a page explaining where the research seems to be going; the next month's presenter may bring an article almost ready to submit to a journal for publication. A member may present several times as a project develops, and it's exciting to see where the group's feedback leads.

THE BENEFITS

Leadership roles in collaborative groups can be very rewarding. The three key strategies presented in this chapter will help leaders effectively manage a group and help them overcome and avoid issues related to organization, motivation, and professionalism of the group. Leaders who are aware of what will cause the group to struggle with organization and how to overcome these struggles are being proactive. Leaders who establish motivational factors will help the group perform at higher levels and are more likely to achieve the goals of the group. Leaders who value professional strengths of members will sustain longevity, which is needed to fulfill the mission or goals of the group.

Part Four presents model learning communities. In Chapter Eight, we will look at school-based and partnership communities.

PART

Model Learning Communities in Action

INTRODUCTION

A COLLABORATIVE EXCHANGE
By Connie Feldt-Golden

*Dedicated to all my students who have shared their stories
as collaborative teacher researchers.*

Had I stifled my students? Grown stale in my teaching,
Concerned for right answers, not the ways and the means?
Each day, it got harder as we struggled for meaning.
I asked a few questions; it was hard on my own.

A peer shared a thought that opened the door
To new understandings and a commitment to grow,
There's dialogue, support, a chance to explore,

We're sharing and learning, no longer alone.
Now students make choices, solve problems, discover,
They share and reflect and construct new ideas.
As teachers, we watch and we listen together
And share in the joy of inspired exchange.

Whether you want to begin a grassroots collaboration or a citywide program, Part Four offers opportunities to think about and consider both. The chapters in this part provide samples of various types of collaborative teacher research groups, such as school-university partnerships and online communities. Technology has opened the possibilities of collaborating and networking with colleagues and potential study participants around the world. According to Papert (1994), the computer has become a learner's technology that helps us feel the power of our individual intellectual personalities.

You will be reading about a number of what Fuhrer (2004) has referred to as "behavior settings" (p. 189). A behavior setting indicates the context of a situation: the location, the people involved, the physical features of the location, the purpose of the group, and any other factors that influence the behaviors and intentions of the members. Fuhrer proposes that to understand the learning and interactions that take place in particular behavior settings, we have to pay close attention to the details of the setting. Therefore, as you are reading these chapters, keep in mind that whichever type of collaborative group you choose to develop or work in, it will contain its own unique attributes; meanings; opportunities; social forces, risks, expectations, and even embarrassments; learning; and encounters. Applying what you learned in Part Two, each type of group will more than likely evolve through its unique composition of group dynamics and communities of practice.

As you read these chapters, reflect on how lines in "A Collaborative Exchange" connect to the examples in these chapters. And how does this collaborative exchange look different and take on different meanings across contexts and behavior settings? For example, if a "peer shared a thought," how might the receiver's interpretation be different in the context of an online collaboration versus in the context of a school-university partnership? The Reflection Questions and Study Group Exercises in Appendixes B and C will help all readers focus on the main points of the chapter.

8

School-Based and Partnership Communities

How to Use This Chapter

This chapter will look at a variety of types of school-based communities but, for reasons described later, will focus in more depth on school-university partnerships. We will also look at the Japanese model of lesson study as a methodology on the rise. This chapter includes two Collaboration at Work features to provide you with excellent examples of working groups: one a neophyte, the other a more established partnership. As you read these features, mark an exclamation point (!) when you read a strategy or idea that you might apply to your group. Jot a question mark (?) in the margin near thoughts about which you want to talk with your group.

Before reading this chapter, reflect on your attempts at teacher research. How might they have benefited from working in some type of collaborative group, such as a school-university partnership? Or how might your teaching benefit from the ongoing support from colleagues through networking and lesson study? Use this chapter to learn about types of collaborations and reflect on the type that is right for your group and your research.

INTRODUCTION

Educators report and write about being part of a variety of types of collaborative teacher research groups. Two such types of teacher research groups are presented in this chapter:

- School-based groups
- School-university partnerships

Each of these groups is unique and offers its members different advantages.

After presenting these two types of groups, we will discuss lesson study, an approach that is becoming widely popular as an alternative type of collaborative teacher research.

SCHOOL-BASED GROUPS

School-based groups usually offer support from colleagues and administrators at a very local level. Educators may be all from the same grade level, from the same school, or from the same district. These folks know each other by face, may have a high degree of comfort in having known each other before the collaboration began, and are more likely to live and work in close proximity to each other, as compared with members of the other types of collaborations we will discuss. This proximity in distance and relationship may promote accelerated development of group dynamics and alleviate some of the conflicts that arise when trying to arrange times and places for meetings.

However, school-based groups may include members from across districts or even states, as we will see in Melissa's story in the following Effective Implementation feature. To reach consensus in decision making, she asked colleagues from a neighboring school district to collaborate with her. The plan was successful and has made quite an impact on both students' and teachers' learning, as you will see.

SCHOOL-UNIVERSITY GROUPS

What is a school-university collaboration? It is an alliance formed between the faculty and administration or staff of a school and professors at a college or university for the purpose of professional development. Some of these relationships have developed through the professional development schools model while others have been sparked by individuals.

Theoretically, all members of the group are involved to learn about teaching and learning. School teachers who completed our survey told us they looked to their university partners to meet a variety of needs, such as

- Framing the study
- Moving through the research process
- Suggesting relevant readings and resources
- Providing a sounding board to process and try out ideas
- Helping to collect data during the school day
- Advising how to sort, code, and analyze data
- Assisting with writing up, disseminating, and even publishing and presenting results

College professors, however, told us they eagerly participate in teacher research collaborations with schools because it allows them to

- Observe and become involved in teaching across grade levels
- Stay abreast of current issues, methods, and strategies in education
- Engage in and learn from conversations with students, classroom teachers, and administrators
- See policies in action

- Learn what equipment and materials are being used in the field
- Make contacts to aid the college's student teaching needs

However, two issues stand out when talking about school-university collaborations. They are the issues of *parity*—equal status—and *power*—equal say, ownership, or control. Is it feasible that the relations between schools and universities can be equal or symmetrical? Can a professor leave behind his or her college culture of the "ivory tower,? How can a classroom teacher nurture collaboration with the professor? Is it realistic or romantic to think that school-university partners can come together and work effectively based on "shared mutual aspirations and a common conceptual framework, (Appley & Winder, 1977, p. 281)? Are they just too different?

Two studies help to shed light on parity and power. Johnston and Kerper (1996) found in their study of these partnerships that those involved in effective school-university teacher research partnerships moved away from "romantic assumptions that they should give up the power assigned to their roles and assimilate into the school-based culture to the realization that they cannot ignore their roles, give up their power, or disregard their university culture. They argue that power has a role in nurturing collaboration and that parity must be more than creating similarities and equality, (p. 5). Johnston and Kerper suggest that instead of giving up power, both participants need to negotiate ways to create it and "to help each other feel powerful in ways that further our individual growth and the relations within the group, (p. 22). Care has to be taken, however, in negotiating power, because intentions are easily misinterpreted. What one person sees as leadership, another may interpret as aggressiveness. The researchers propose goals not unlike those presented in Chapter Two: they encourage frank, open conversations that challenge positions and interpretations. After all, what makes us feel more powerful than being heard and understood and seeing our ideas being implemented or contribution being considered?

Yet another study of parity and power in school-university partnerships, by Baumfield and Butterworth (2007), seemingly contradicts the findings of Johnston and Kerper (1996). Baumfield and Butterworth (2007) tell us from their recent study of fifty-one schools that in such a setting, the research project dissolves the tension between an impetus for bonding and the flexibility of bridging across the school-university social networks. They see this model as "fruitful in unraveling the relationship between theory and practice in the pursuit of knowledge about teaching and learning, (p. 411).

We have presented both sides to the story, because in our own work and in the responses to our surveys we have experienced this fruitful unraveling and the necessity to maintain roles and cultures across contexts. We don't see one as exclusive of the other. They actually complement each other. The answer may lie among the attributes or expectations of all parties involved. For example, if a school invites a college to collaborate with them, they may be expecting the college professors to maintain the school's culture. Expecting the college to meet teachers' needs may require professors to maintain and demonstrate their roles as experts in a certain field of research. Relying on this expertise may perpetuate the college culture because conversations lead to research or extended reading the professor has done on the topic. The unraveling occurs when together the teacher (practice) and professor (theory) share a common goal: to improve students' learning.

From another perspective, if a professor approaches a teacher to participate in a classroom environment, the professor may be thinking she will be part of the classroom. In reality this

THINKING TOGETHER: INVITING THE IN-LAWS

There is something challenging about inviting someone into your environment. Even having your in-laws over for the holidays, especially when they become overnight guests, can feel in many ways intrusive to your daily routine and the comfort of your home. As much as you welcome their company, you may heave a sigh of relief when the holidays are over and your household is back to normal.

When research designs include "inviting the in-laws"—in this case research colleagues—into your classroom for an extended stay to assist with data collection, you are probably not the only one who will feel or act differently than you would under normal circumstances. Students may behave different from normal, which may skew the results of the study. The teacher may be hesitant to correct students' inappropriate behavior so as not to draw attention to it or not to appear unpleasant. Or the teacher may act more strictly than usual to appear in control of the class. We have only to think back to our student teaching days when the college supervisor stepped into the room to be able to relate to the stress of having an invited guest in our classrooms. We may feel we are being evaluated even if that isn't the purpose of the visit and even if that guest is the teacher from down the hall.

We should consider the following:

- How the presence of "the in-laws" influences the behaviors and, most important, the learning of the student participants
- How to build trusting and respectful relationships among all involved
- How to maintain confidentiality and safe environments for all

does not always happen. In her description of her first experience in a classroom as part of a college research team, a colleague explained to me that she expected the students to warm up to her as they did when she was an elementary classroom teacher. However, she soon found that students' loyalties remained with their teacher. She remained to them the woman from the college, which was a disappointing realization for my friend (Ware, Mallozzi, Edwards, & Baumann, 2008).

In *Teachers Taking Action: A Comprehensive Guide to Teacher Research*, Ware, Mallozzi, Edwards, and Baumann (Lassonde & Israel, 2008) list these tips for collaborative teacher researchers from their work in school-university partnerships:

- Identify co-researchers you know and trust and with whom you have common interests.
- Construct and refine research questions that address the interests of all researchers.
- Determine goals for division of labor up front, knowing that these may need to be revised. Talk about who will provide the instruction, gather data, analyze data, and draft reports.
- Discuss authorship order and how it may rotate across papers and presentations.
- Communicate often and candidly regarding the planning and implementation of the study (pp. 98–99).

Next, read Parts A, B, and C of this chapter's first Collaboration at Work feature. Each part shares a district's Informed Teaching Through Inquiry initiative. Developed to enhance professional development in the district, the initiative involved forming a partnership between K–12 teachers in Mt. Markham Central Schools and a group of professors from the Division of Education at the SUNY College at Oneonta. Voices from both the school and the college are represented. In this first Collaboration at Work feature, you will learn how this group collaborated to begin their partnership. Also, in Part C, the author connects personal prior experiences in the field of science and theory from the world of business to her work with Mt. Markham. Then, in this chapter's second Collaboration at Work feature, you will hear about an established team's partnership. From reading these two Collaboration at Work features in this chapter, you not only learn from others' experiences with beginning a very grassroots partnership but also from a more experienced team's methods of maintaining and growing a more extensive partnership. Both are very valuable opportunities to investigate and reflect upon.

COLLABORATION AT WORK 1

Part A: Building Informed Teaching Through Inquiry

Contributed by Lynne Burns, district literacy coach, Mt. Markham Central School District

In October 2006, at the annual New York State English Council Conference in Albany, New York, I attended a workshop focusing on the subject of teacher research presented by Cynthia Lassonde, a literacy professor at SUNY College at Oneonta. Participants discussed the benefits of using teacher research with in-service teachers.

When I returned to MMCSD and shared the ideas from the workshop, the Mt. Markham superintendent, Casey Barduhn, decided to explore teacher research further as a way to continue building a professional learning community in the district. An inquiry process that would support teachers who used research and classroom data to inform teaching choices seemed worthwhile.

In November, Casey and I met with Cynthia and a couple of her colleagues to talk about the viability of bringing teacher research to MMCSD. Casey and I left the college campus with a desire to continue exploring teacher research at Mt. Markham and, in February 2007, established a teacher panel to give it further consideration. The panel consisted of teachers representing each of the buildings in the district—elementary (Grades Pre-K through 4), middle (5 through 8), and high school (9 through 12), the superintendent, and me, the district literacy coach.

The Teacher Research Panel met several times over the early spring of 2007 to determine whether the idea of teacher research was worth pursuing and, if so, the best design for MMCSD. Initially, the panel focused on the question "What is teacher research?" Only one of the teachers had actually completed a research project as part of graduate school requirements. The panel studied introductory chapters of several teacher research texts and read materials collected by the professors in the college's teacher research classes. By the end of the first meeting, the panel had shared many

(continued)

(continued)

reasons why teacher research would be useful to teachers (for example, "It is a way to create our own data—for us," or "It will lead to best practices. It is classroom centered, specific to a teacher's classroom," or "It will give information between tests") and many questions and concerns (such as "Is it voluntary?" or "Is it for everyone?" and "This must happen in a safe environment"). The consensus was that some form of teacher research would be useful to offer at Mt. Markham.

The next time the panel met was to discuss "How do we bring teacher research to Mt. Markham?" Panel members considered many questions including: What could a research project look like? How could the district support the program and participants? Would teachers earn in-service credit? Could the project be part of New York State's mandated Annual Professional Performance Review (APPR)? What would be the role of the principals? The Union? How and when do the college professors become involved?

On May 1, 2007, the Mt. Markham Teacher Research Panel visited the college campus to talk with graduate students after they presented their current research work. (Read more about this campus meeting in Part B of this feature by Connie Feldt-Golden.) The panel also met with professors who were supporting Mt. Markham in its project. We continued to focus on implementation questions such as: Is there a basic, simple process that researchers can use to focus, gather, and analyze data? What might the relationship between the college and Mt. Markham look like?

In early June the Mt. Markham Teacher Research Panel and a group of professors met at Mt. Markham High School to discuss progress to date and how, when, and where the idea of using classroom research to inform classroom choices could be presented to the entire professional staff. At this time, the group began to look closely at any ethical, legal, and policy issues related to teacher research in public classrooms. A final summer meeting in August put the finishing touches on a brief presentation to the entire Mt. Markham staff on the first day of school. It was at that meeting that the panel members decided to call the research process Informed Teaching Through Inquiry, or ITTI for short.

In late August, the superintendent and a panel member introduced the entire faculty to the idea of ITTI and how it could connect to in-service credits and the APPR. Interested teachers were invited to attend a follow-up meeting on September 17 with the Teaching Through Inquiry Panel and representatives from SUNY. About a dozen teachers and a building administrator attended. After a presentation of basic information about ITTI, attendees engaged in an extended period of "mingling" to share essential questions, answers, and concerns and to peruse handout materials that included case studies of actual classroom research. By the end of this meeting, eight people had signed up. Each participant designated a topic in which he or she was interested, as well as a desire to be contacted by one of the Oneonta representatives.

The Mt. Markham District continues to support the teacher researchers as each of them partners with a member of the SUNY group and begins the work of honing a researchable question, collecting data in the classroom, and eventually, applying their research to instructional decisions.

ROLES

In building a partnership and camaraderie among SUNY and Mt. Markham, teachers will benefit from the experience, knowledge, and expertise that the college staff brings. Mt. Markham teachers will deepen their connection to the broader professional world and have access to ideas and research to inform their teaching. In exchange, Mt. Markham can offer SUNY professors an opportunity to share time with our teachers and experience their day-to-day challenges and needs. This time spent with in-service K–12 teachers may give SUNY staff further insights in teaching aspiring teachers how they can use the inquiry process. Working with MMCSD teachers will offer an opportunity for the Oneonta faculty and students a chance to observe and gain insight from experienced and master classroom teachers. SUNY College at Oneonta and Mt. Markham staff will provide support for each other as we explore the inquiry process.

PLANS FOR THE FUTURE

Our overarching goal at Mt. Markham is to continue to build and support a Professional Learning Community. ITTI can be one branch on which to build that community. Teacher research can help Mt. Markham develop its internal capacity by encouraging teachers to use their own interests and questions to drive inquiry and apply their learning in the classroom. At the same time, as teachers draw on good ideas from a research community beyond our school walls to address that inquiry process, they will engage with previously unknown or untried ideas. Along with making more conscious, research-based classroom choices, there is increased potential for Mt. Markham teachers who participate in ITTI to build professional support networks among themselves, cutting across the classroom and bridging boundaries that may exist.

It is our hope that the ITTI design will continue to be revised by teachers from Mt. Markham and SUNY Oneonta so that it meets the unique needs of our staff. We would like to see an increasing number of Mt. Markham teachers participate in this process each year and use inquiry and research to drive instructional decisions. We hope that as the SUNY Oneonta staff continues to develop a working relationship with day-to-day life at Mt. Markham, they will have the opportunity to see what the material they teach in college classrooms actually looks like in the K–12 classrooms.

We look forward to the time when it will be the norm that Mt. Markham classroom teachers and SUNY Oneonta staff meet and greet each other in the school halls. "Oh, them?" teachers might answer a visitor. "Those are the Oneonta professors. They're part of our Professional Learning Community."

Part B: Generating Powerful Connections
Contributed by Connie Feldt-Golden, department chair, SUNY College at Oneonta

Hearing about the Mt. Markham teachers' interest in exploring action research generated lots of excitement on our campus. Here was an opportunity for education faculty to brainstorm with K–12 teachers and share in the process of classroom discovery.

(continued)

(continued)

To get the ball rolling, we looked at the teacher action research project required in our current graduate programs. The last two courses in our Master's in Education programs focus on students designing, implementing, and analyzing action research studies in K–12 classrooms. Given that most of our graduate students are practicing teachers, it seemed appropriate to share their reflections of the project as a first step in brainstorming possibilities. We met the Mt. Markham superintendent and literacy coach for the first time during the middle of the fall 2006 semester. Some informational data that we had collected on our own programs revealed that graduate students valued doing projects that entailed working with their students and discovering how research can help students learn more effectively. We shared these comments with the Mt. Markham administrators, and they clearly saw the benefits of the research project for our graduate students in terms of professional growth, and recognized the parallel possibilities for their own teachers. A powerful connection was made that day between teacher research and professional development on all levels (K–16), and a collaborative, collegial connection was made between Mt. Markham and SUNY Oneonta in pursuing the possibilities.

A follow-up meeting with a group of Oneonta faculty and Mt. Markham teachers and administrators took place near the end of the spring 2007 semester. Professors and teachers met as a group to share individual goals and backgrounds. Two very enthusiastic graduate students (one elementary teacher and one high school teacher) briefly presented their research projects, specifically as to how they got started and what they found. This exchange highlighted the power of teacher research. Teachers were talking to teachers and sharing their excitement about bringing innovative ideas into the reality of their classrooms. The enthusiasm was catching! Then the entire group attended the research poster session where graduate students described the designs of their upcoming research projects. Questions were raised, ideas were shared, new insights were gained. A spirit of collaboration filled the room, and it was very exciting! It appeared that both groups, graduate students and Mt. Markham teachers alike, were invigorated by each other's participation. Connections were made as graduate students and teachers converged in plans for best practice.

The next fall semester, the conversation continued. Five Oneonta faculty members joined several Mt. Markham teachers in an information panel to address a group of Mt. Markham teachers considering becoming involved in the initiative. It was gratifying to discover that one of the teachers in the group was one of our own graduate students who had completed a teacher action research project only a few years earlier.

The Oneonta faculty and Mt. Markham teachers shared their areas of interest (literacy, mathematics, science) and then the small-group informal discussions began. Elements of curriculum, instruction, and assessment were all discussed as teachers looked beyond their current teaching behaviors to institute a positive effect on their students' learning and motivation. But it takes time to pick each other's brains, and we know that time is always a challenge in the busy lives of teachers. Teachers exchanged e-mail addresses and enough of a connection was made that first day for several pairs to start brainstorming online. The partnership had truly begun.

For so long, teachers have been regarded only as unenthusiastic consumers of educational research. As demonstrated by our graduate students and the teachers from the MMCSD, action research seems to assist teachers in connecting theory and practice and in performing the dual role of researcher and reflective practitioner, a role inherent in day-to-day teaching. The challenge for us as MMCSD's university partner is to promote that connection as we continue to work together and grow this partnership.

Part C: Reflecting on Lessons Learned

Contributed by Leanne Avery, assistant professor, SUNY College at Oneonta

As one of the original SUNY faculty members of the Informed Teaching Through Inquiry initiative (ITTI), I have been able to witness firsthand our process of creating a community of learners. Like many university-school partnerships before ours, we struggle with the growing pains of putting a mechanism like this in place. We are experiencing the joy and enthusiasm the members have in engaging in this process and, at the same time, we are cognizant of the potential barriers and issues as they arise. As I have been participating in our process, I have found myself reflecting both on specific past experiences with building and sustaining communities of practice (COP) and on several literature bases that shed light on the issues we have been facing.

These literatures include institutional theory, communities of practice (COP), and science education and university-school science collaborations. Each offers insights regarding "lessons learned," a theoretical base in which to frame and understand the issues we are facing, and suggestions for ways to sustain and grow our COP. I frame each ITTI issue in the context of the appropriate literature base below.

INSTITUTIONAL THEORY AND THE PERSISTENCE OF SCHOOLS

Perhaps one of the more important things to recognize at the onset of an initiative is the nature of public schools and the context in which we are trying to create this collaboration. As mentioned earlier, we have already explored the "ivory tower" issues that sometimes come with working with faculty. But what we haven't explored is the institutional nature of schools that make forming this collaboration more challenging. These institutional factors do not necessarily reflect the dedication and engagement of the individual teachers, college faculty, and the superintendent, all of whom are working hard to create this particular collaboration, but rather, reflect the overall persistence in the way schools as organizations have historically functioned.

For decades, schools have been very successful at maintaining continuity and constancy. They have perfected mechanisms for preserving their stability and making sure that what happens today will happen again tomorrow and the next day, and so on (Cuban, 1992). All levels of the school organization—the district, school, administrators, and teachers—have perfected routines and practices to detect and buffer the "noise" in their immediate environments (Cuban, 1992). Societal institutions in general create and maintain social order by providing roles, expectations, norms, and ways of thinking (Sipple, 1997). According to scholars in institutional theory, an institutional

(continued)

(continued)

environment is described as the external pressures (such as rules, norms, and belief systems or, in the case of schools, test scores and public and community perception for example) that influence a given organization (Sipple, 1997).

The school environment is no different. Mechanisms have evolved over the years that protect the technical core—the teaching in the classroom—from the external environment. Historically, little research or investigation has happened beyond the classroom door. Prior to No Child Left Behind (NCLB), teachers were left to practice their craft. Obtaining local and state resources now requires schools to pay close attention to the details of their externally assessed formal structure. For example, a great deal of energy is spent on attending to the details of management: allocation of resources, space, materials, scheduling, classes, attendance, and the basic structural components that allow the school to function on a daily basis. This practice of attending to external assessments that create the school's organizational structure is, according to Meyer and Rowan (1977), engaging in the *myth and ceremony* of ritual classification and practices.

Schools have achieved a balance between maintaining their external legitimacy and keeping instruction shielded from change. However, there is often conflict between conforming to institutional rules and maintaining efficiency. Therefore, educational organizations have adopted a means by which to achieve this balance—a means of buffering between ceremonial structure and technical activity—called *loose coupling* (Meyer & Rowan 1975, 1977; Weick 1976). Meyer and Rowan (1975) describe loose coupling as follows:

> *Institutional products, services, techniques, policies, and programs function as powerful myths, and many organizations adopt them ceremonially. But conformity to institutionalized rules often conflicts sharply with efficiency criteria and, conversely, to coordinate and control activity in order to promote efficiency undermines an organization's ceremonial conformity, organizations that reflect institutional rules tend to buffer their formal structures from the uncertainties of technical activities by becoming loosely coupled, building gaps between their formal structures and actual work activities. (p. 341)*

NCLB has put significant restraints on schools in response to loose coupling and has had the result of driving less than best practices in classrooms. Measures of accountability have forced many teachers to teach to the test. Teachers' proclivity to pursue more creative endeavors or to explore opportunities to implement inquiry in their classrooms has been dampened by administrative pressures associated with NCLB.

Although we are extremely fortunate to have such a unique and passionate group of teachers and the superintendent from MMCSD, having a full understanding of the school environment and the added pressures of NCLB makes us more aware of the reluctance teachers may have to become involved. On the flip side, because we understand the demands of the current school environment, we can then also see the dedication and passion of those who choose to participate. Therefore, when the issue of how to fit this professional development of teacher inquiry into the MMCSD context arose for us, we were not surprised by the amount of time it took to negotiate what we were going to name our group. There was a clear sense that using the "R" word or "research" in any part of our title or in any flyer or presentation to the larger teacher group was a definite "no-no." Members of the group expressed concern that using the "R" word would be scary and intimidating for teachers. (In addition, I am wondering if using the "R" word didn't evoke fears that the data would indicate that a particular practice was not effective.) Understanding the nature of the school organization and utilizing it as the backdrop, it makes sense that this naming process was an important one that needed to be treated delicately. One veteran teacher who had been integral in the planning of the collaboration summarized it quite nicely by saying,

> We don't want to hoodwink them; we want to attract them. If we hide questions away, we aren't attracting the people who will be comfortable with this. At this moment they might not have that innate inquiry. We want to find out what souls will be interested in to be successful with it. [There are some] who are seeking community and professional growth. Ask questions that appeal to feelings [and] you'll get people who come to this because they're feeling they want to be empowered or had a safe place to talk about things. They want to know there is a support group. (Terri, personal communication, June 7, 2007)

Terri also raises another issue here: fear and the need to feel safe. Other teachers in the community also discussed a need for a safe environment to voice concerns and a need to feel safe exploring inquiry. Because these are key concerns, how the group presented this initiative to the larger teacher faculty was paramount. How ITTI can address the issues of fear and safety will be discussed later in the section on lessons learned from the science community.

Other issues that have arisen include logistics and contracts. Quite a bit of time was spent in several meetings regarding the logistics of how to present and represent the concept of teacher inquiry to the broader community. Here, the discussion focused on what exactly should go into the handouts, flyer, and oral presentation at both the initial superintendent's day meeting and the follow-up smaller teacher inquiry meeting for interested teachers. As previously mentioned, language was incredibly important, as was clarity, and making the message simple but not too vague.

In terms of contractual agreements, ITTI teachers raised the topic of using teacher inquiry associated with ITTI as a way of obtaining credit for the district's professional development. What seems to be a logical request also had permeations of what we observe in the institutional theory literature regarding norms and expectations. This contract concern also addressed related fears and potential concerns of teachers regarding the constraints of time, accountability, and engaging in extra projects in addition to the requirements of their jobs. Having a mechanism where inquiry will "count" enables teachers to fit it into an already demanding schedule.

COP LITERATURE

On top of these institutional pressures, it is also important to recognize that creating, sustaining, and growing a COP is not trivial (Avery & Carlsen, 2001). It requires that the participants have equity in the partnership, shared goals, and long-term commitment. According to Wenger (1998), a COP is comprised of three elements: a repertoire, shared enterprise, and mutual engagement:

(continued)

(continued)

> The repertoire of a community of practice includes routines, works, tools, ways of doing things, stories, gestures, symbols, genres, actions, or concepts that the community has produced or adopted in the course of its existence, and which have become part of its practice. The repertoire combines both reificative and participative aspects. It includes the discourse by which members create meaningful statements about the world, as well as the styles by which they express their forms of membership and their identities as members. (p. 83)

> These practices are the property of a kind of community created over time by the sustained pursuit of a joint enterprise (p. 45). It results from a collective process of negotiation, it is defined by its participants, and it is beyond just a stated goal—that is, it creates among participants a mutual accountability that become an integral part of the practice. (p. 78)

> The first characteristic of practice as the source of coherence of a community is the mutual engagement of participants. Practice does not exist in the abstract. It exists because people are engaged in actions whose meanings they negotiate with one another . . . Practice resides in a community of people and the relations of mutual engagement by which they can do whatever they do. Membership and community of practice is therefore a matter of mutual engagement. That is what defines a community. (p. 73)

The ITTI seems to demonstrate all three of these criteria. We have an established repertoire that includes members taking on various roles and identities; attention to language and representation of who we are; and the practices that define us. For example, at our meetings, Lynne, the district literacy coach, is clearly the leader who initiated this collaboration and continues to pave the way along with Casey, the superintendent. Terri offers in-depth thought on research possibilities, potential teacher concerns, and often articulates solutions to these issues by proposing to create informative PowerPoint presentations, flyers, and other helpful suggestions. Elaine is often the voice that represents teachers who may need to know that they have a safe place to ask questions, discuss, and share ideas about their potential projects. Chris, one of our former graduate students, represents the voice of experience, sharing with the group insights about the process and offering herself as a resource. These are the roles and identities that define our group.

This discussion about fear surrounding the use of the "R" word also signifies the use of terminology in our repertoire as does the culture and conversation surrounding professional development. Our understanding of this repertoire is essential for the success of the project.

Although we are still in the process of defining our practices, over time we have established a core group of teachers, superintendent, and Oneonta faculty who are committed to pursuing our shared enterprise of creating a community of learners in professional development regarding teacher inquiry.

The mutual engagement of the community works because there is equity and parity among the members, which allows people to be engaged in actions whose meanings they negotiate with one another (Wenger, 1998).

Thus far, we have partnered faculty with teachers, which is a good step in the right direction. However, it seems that to fully engage teachers in ITTI, we need to consider investing in more structured programs to help teachers feel safe, confident, and ready to implement inquiry in their classrooms.

In summary, as we look to the future, we can find support in literature bases that better help us to understand the context we are in and also give us ideas or lessons learned to facilitate building our ITTI community.

THINKING TOGETHER: SCHOOL-UNIVERSITY PARTNERSHIPS

Contributed by Taffy E. Raphael and Susan R. Goldman

For much of our professional lives, we have participated as members of school-university partnerships designed to generate knowledge and improve educational practices. For example, Taffy's partnerships in southeastern Michigan, such as the Teachers Learning Collaborative (Goatley, Highfield, Bentley, et al., 1994) and the Book Club Plus Curriculum Network (Raphael, Florio-Ruane, Kehus, et al., 2001), focused on constructing the Book Club curriculum and extending that work to create a framework for differentiating instruction for learners with diverse needs. Susan's work in Schools for Thought in Nashville, Tennessee, centered on integrating contemporary principles of teaching, learning, and assessment with technology-supported, guided-inquiry approaches to instruction (Goldman, 2005; Lamon, Secules, Petrosino, et al., 1996; Secules, Cottom, Bray, & Miller, 1997). Over the ten-year period of this work, Susan worked to create partnerships between university researchers and individual teachers, schools, and the district as a whole.

We arrived at the University of Illinois at Chicago (UIC) in 2001 and through fortunate timing of a new initiative in the city called the Advanced Reading Development Demonstration Project (ARDDP, 2008) became members of a unique partnership among six Chicago-area universities, the largest community foundation in Chicago (the Chicago Community Trust), and the Chicago Public Schools. Our part of this collaboration is the UIC-based Partnership READ (Reading Essentials and Assessment Development). The team includes faculty, staff, and graduate students from the College of Education along with the staffs (principals, literacy coordinators, classroom teachers) of Chicago elementary schools who elect to participate in the work. We limit the number of participating schools to ten each year; new schools join the collaboration as space becomes available. The collaboration involves schools that have partnered with us from one to six years. Partnership READ focuses on improving literacy teaching and learning within the district by building capacity in the schools and by connecting UIC's teacher education and professional development programs and coursework directly to teachers' practices and the needs of the administrators, curriculum leaders, teachers, and students in Chicago Public Schools.

In our work within Partnership READ, we are learning a great deal about how to create successful school-university partnerships that benefit members in both settings. We share three

(continued)

(continued)

interrelated lessons that we believe are fundamental to successful and productive partnerships. They are to:

1. Plan to work at multiple levels over multiple years
2. Approach change as an iterative, inquiry process
3. Take advantage of opportunities to address both university- and school-based problems of practice

Lesson 1. Plan to Work at Multiple Levels over Multiple Years

Successful school-university partnerships take seriously the multiple, embedded contexts that comprise the educational system and work collaboratively within and across these levels over time (McLaughlin & Talbert, 1993). Within a school, work is conducted with individual teachers, grade-level teams, whole faculties, and school leaders. The school itself is part of within-district organizational structures and is subject to district mandates. These local contexts exist within state and national contexts that often set policies on funding and accountability and have an impact on which content is included and how teaching and learning are conducted within schools and classrooms. For example, the READ school-university partnership's agreed-on overall goal is improving schoolwide literacy achievement. Achieving that goal involves generating smaller aligned goals that are shared across school and university partners. Implementing a change in processes to achieve the goals must involve the entire professional community in reflecting on current practice; analyzing school strengths and challenges; and enhancing relevant knowledge in literacy, leadership, and the school change process providing the backbone for Partnership READ (for example, the Standards-Based Change [SBC] Process developed by Kathy Au [Au, 2005; Au, Raphael, & Mooney, in press a]).

"Local" goals of the partnership must accommodate district goals. Some of the district goals reflect responses to state and national policies or funding, even if these goals do not align with local goals. For example, early in the partnership, the district mandated that all READ schools apply for Reading First funds. On the surface, this seemed well aligned with READ goals (such as improving achievement); in actuality it was not. Time and effort demands for writing the grants and enacting the Reading First policies competed with READ activities for schools' limited time and resources, especially time for teachers to work together and participate in professional development activities targeting the SBC Process. Further, state- and district-mandated goals for Reading First emphasized early primary grades, whereas local goals related to the SBC Process involved the whole school.

This example underscores the importance of working across multiple levels—creating highly functional communication systems at every level to ensure that the goals of all initiatives enacted in a school align with one another, address the local needs identified through the process of self-analysis and reflection, build on a school's strengths, and address challenges to a school's success. And consistent with lessons learned from work with individual teachers in changing their practice, aligning goals and enacting effective change processes across levels occurs over time—often years. READ partners committed to working together across several years. We began in fall 2002 and, in our most successful schools, partnered for at least three to six years, with local goals and implementation activities changing across time (see Au, Raphael, & Mooney, in press b).

LESSON 2. APPROACH CHANGE AS AN ITERATIVE INQUIRY PROCESS

Change over time occurs in cycles of planning, implementation, reflection, and revision, whether working to improve children's classroom experiences, teachers' practices, or professional development. That is, to achieve learning goals, teachers at both the classroom and whole-school levels need to plan instruction based on examining evidence of what students are learning. Similarly, university staff members need to examine evidence of impact of their work on students, teachers, and the schools. The inquiry process provides critical feedback for continuous improvement of the activities and implementation processes intended to enhance instructional processes and outcomes.

In Partnership READ, the inquiry orientation has been critical to internal changes that schools made and to changes that university staff made in their support activities and tools. For example, schools created new infrastructures to increase communication and functional work times for school teams to promote coherence and alignment of end-of-year literacy learning goals within and across grade levels and subject areas. Initial efforts revealed the need for new evidence systems for ongoing analysis of students' progress toward end-of-year goals and opportunities to share results in whole-school events at key points in the academic year. Schools established "Gallery Walks" that took place three times per year in which each grade level or subject team shared their end-of-year targets, agreed-on classroom-embedded assessments used to track students' progress, ways of scoring these assessments to point to instructional needs, and instructional plans based on the results. They analyzed the entire event for evidence of strengths and challenges for their school's professional community and for evidence of a coherent literacy curriculum that supported students' progress across time.

For the university staff, one way in which inquiry cycles played out was in biweekly debriefing "school update" sessions. The updates detailed activities and outcomes of work to date in each school and determined what specific support to provide to individual schools, grade levels, or teachers. Further, evidence across school updates resulted in the university staff creating tools (for example, Analyzing a Gallery Walk: A Guide to Effective Grade Level Meetings) for use in professional development, and instruments for analyzing and guiding school progress (such as Needs Assessment). The Needs Assessment, based on Au's analysis (2005) of schools' progress in Hawai'i and the ARDDP's (2008) analysis of progress in Chicago schools, helped university staff to organize and present evidence to schools that illustrated their progress on their efforts toward creating their functional infrastructure, improving classroom practices, and increasing students' engagement and achievement.

LESSON 3. ADDRESS UNIVERSITY-BASED AS WELL AS SCHOOL-BASED PROBLEMS OF PRACTICE

Partnerships provide opportunities to identify problems of practice for all sectors of participants. Just as Johnston and Kerper (1996) stress valuing knowledge in both K–12 and university sectors, participants from each sector can learn from one another to improve practice in both. As demonstrated in the K–12 sector, change processes are most effective when they address

(continued)

(continued)

practitioner-identified problems of practice. Such problems of practice are often "close" to the school, classroom, or students. Similarly, in the university education sector, problems of practice are close to the program, the course, or education students. In both contexts, when efforts to change practice are cast as inquiry, problems of practice can emerge and solutions can be developed and tested.

For example, university literacy faculty members traditionally offer formal graduate coursework leading to degrees, certification, or endorsement or provide formal or informal coursework through district professional development activities. Yet, neither model addressed the needs of our K–8 partners. Although an explicit district and school goal was to increase the number of highly qualified reading teachers (for example, those with a state reading endorsement or reading specialist certification), obtaining these qualifications through the existing university channels did not seem to be contributing to the larger goal of building teacher literacy leadership capacity in the schools.

In response to this problem of practice, the university staff created a hybrid program, Partnership READ Fellows. Principals nominated potential teacher leaders for the Fellows program and the program provided professional development experiences that integrated formal coursework in literacy methods and leadership with school-based SBC Process initiatives. The program emphasized Fellow's practitioner inquiry to address specific problems of practice within their classrooms. Culminating course events provided public opportunities for sharing their inquiries with their peers and colleagues, the annual Fellows Inquiry and Strategy Conference.

The Ultimate Goal

Finally, what we hope to achieve for school-university collaboration is to eliminate any barriers across the two contexts so that, as partners, we can promote deep learning and engagement to solve important issues in literacy education for diverse learners. We have learned that it is critical to work across levels, taking an inquiry stance to address key problems of practice. We know that we are achieving our goal when the lines between "them" in the schools and "us" in the university are blurred. Thus, most rewarding to us are comments like the one recently made by one of our principals at the beginning of a Gallery Walk at which university staff were present. She was reassuring her staff that this was a time for openness and honesty since, in her words, "There's nobody here but *us*" (Gallery Walk, video, September 2007).

Lesson Study

The last type of collaborative teacher research group we would like to share with you is lesson study. Ann Taylor and Barbara O'Donnell do a wonderful job explaining this method in this chapter's Collaboration at Work 2.

COLLABORATION AT WORK 2

What Is Lesson Study?

Contributed by Ann R. Taylor and Barbara D. O'Donnell

Lesson study (Lewis, 2002) is a professional development process used widely in Japan. Groups of four to six teachers work through a collaborative cycle of inquiry: (1) setting a teaching goal; (2) teaching and observing together a lesson they have planned in great detail; (3) discussing this enacted lesson and raising questions about their students' learning and their pedagogical choices based on the evidence they have gathered; and (4) reflecting and concluding, and if they choose, starting the process over again.

Having worked through the lesson study process with teachers over the last eight years, we would offer these ideas to make your own work a success.

Use Electronic Resources to Help You

Thousands of teachers are doing lesson study across the country: often in school district–supported groups, sometimes through collaborating with a university, sometimes through grants, and sometimes in independent groups of like-minded teachers. There are a few groups who teach their research lesson and invite the public to be observers throughout the teaching and debriefing process. Check to see what is available in your geographic area. Commit yourselves to enjoying exploring the resources. Take the plunge and ask your questions on a listserv. These four Web links will guide you right into the heart of lesson study and provide all the resources you need to get going or develop your group!

1. Lesson Study Group at Mills College, Oakland, California

   www.lessonresearch.net
   One of the main centers for resources and research on lesson study in the United States, this group has been working with public school teachers on lesson study since the late 1990s. Spend time with the resources Web page. There are reasonably priced videos and DVDs of teachers carrying out lesson study ($15–35); free handouts and worksheets to help you in the planning and teaching process; articles about teachers taking part in lesson study; sample lesson plans from lesson studies; and much more.

2. Teachers College, Columbia University Lesson Study Group, New York

   www.tc.edu/centers/lessonstudy
   Hosted by the other major research center for lesson study in the United States, this site also provides excellent information and free handouts to guide you through the process.

3. E-mail discussion list

   http://mailman.depaul.edu/mailman/listinfo/lsnetwork

(*continued*)

(continued)

> This e-mail listserv, initiated by Akihiko Takahashi—a Japanese educator from DePaul University specializing in lesson study—is for lesson study practitioners just like you. You will find announcements of upcoming lesson study events, be able to share results of your lesson study, and direct your questions to other lesson study practitioners.

4. Company offering resources about lesson study
   www.globaledresources.com/
   Global Education Resources is a private company founded by Makoto Yoshida, a Japanese educator, author, and expert in lesson study. The company mission includes education about lesson study and their Web site includes links to other lesson study groups in the United States.

Try a Study Group or Book Club to Get You Started

As previously recommended in this book, a study-group or book-club format can help you learn about lesson study for a few months before you dive into the process. We would recommend these books:

Lewis, C. (2002). *Lesson study: A handbook of teacher-led instructional change.* Philadelphia, PA: Research for Better Schools.

Stepanek, J., Appel, G., Leong, M., Mangan, M. T., & Mitchell, M. (2007). *Leading lesson study: A practical guide for leaders and facilitators.* Thousand Oaks, CA: Corwin.

Take Goal Setting (AKA Your "Research Theme") Seriously

This goal setting is different from all the attention to standards. What do you really hope your students will be like in five years' time? Most teachers we know say things like: "I dream of them becoming independent learners, who are also able to work cooperatively with others to solve problems." Lesson study gives you permission to discuss and agree on a common goal or research theme with your colleagues. This goal then guides your detailed lesson planning: if you cannot decide which direction to take in a lesson, or which resource to use, then ask yourselves: "Which way will fulfill our goal?" The goal setting is surprisingly hard to do, both for novices and experts alike, but what an opportunity to begin to return to some of your deepest purposes for teaching, and plan a lesson that brings these goals to life.

Planning Will Take You Much Longer Than You Think

We have found this to be the biggest shock for those new to lesson study. ("How can planning a lesson possibly take us ten hours set? I can rip through a plan in fifteen minutes max.") In order to plan a lesson that can be analyzed, it needs to include many negotiated details as well as deep thought about the concept being taught, so allow yourselves about two-thirds of your time to plan that "research lesson." You will also benefit from working through the lesson content from a student perspective to avoid surprises.

SCHEDULE MEETINGS, BUT TALK ANY TIME

Schedule a formal time to meet to do all the planning and talking for your lesson study; however, teachers tell us they are surprised to find themselves talking to each other throughout the day about the issues in their lesson: they talk in the teacher's lounge, in the hallway, just about anywhere they encounter each other. They talk about tiny details ("Should we use blue or black markers?" "Would groups of three or four work better?"); they also talk about key ideas ("I just realized: this lesson is about number sense, not place value!").

See Table 8.1 for a clear description of what lesson study is and what it is not.

TABLE 8.1. *Sorting Out Some Misunderstandings*

Lesson Study IS	Lesson Study IS NOT	Comment
Collaborating, discussing, thinking about, and studying teaching and learning with colleagues.	NOT everyone doing part of the process on their own, then putting parts together.	Talking and finding similarities and differences is the point. These ideas will challenge you to understand your practice in different ways.
Improving your teaching of a difficult part of the curriculum.	NOT teaching a "showy" lesson to make you look good.	If a lesson works well, leave it alone. Pick a concept that is hard for students to learn or a lesson that challenges your teaching. You will learn more—about your students and yourselves as teachers.
Studying how students actually learn or struggle when a carefully planned lesson is taught.	NOT about evaluating how a colleague teaches.	Whoever teaches the lesson uses the plan everyone agreed to, so it's a group plan. The focus is on how students learn and the improvement of learning.
Staying with the plan as much as you can. Too many sudden changes while teaching do not provide you with a chance to find out how learning happens.	NOT improvising as the lesson progresses.	If you spend so long planning, presumably you all think that the lesson will help students learn. Find out if it does or does not, and which moments are problems, then discuss the evidence to work out why: this is what lesson study is for.

(continued)

TABLE 8.1. *Sorting Out Some Misunderstandings (continued)*

Lesson Study IS	Lesson Study IS NOT	Comment
Slowing down the process of planning and teaching to study the fine points.	NOT meant to be a planning process you duplicate in your regular school day.	Teaching is fast paced. During a normal school day, a teacher does not have the time to stop and reflect in depth on student learning and teaching. Lesson study permits you to take the time to study and reflect.
Preparing one well-developed "research lesson."	NOT a quick way to develop sets of perfect lesson plans you can all use.	Lesson study does not provide you with perfect lessons. Every class has different needs so one lesson does not work for every fourth grade class. Lesson study helps you study the particulars of teaching and learning.
Improving the teaching of any subject area	NOT just about studying math teaching.	Mathematics got a head start in the United States with lesson study, so many more resources and examples are available, but our teachers use it in science, social studies, and language arts.

Correspondence concerning this information should be addressed to Ann R. Taylor, Box 1122, Department of Curriculum and Instruction, Southern Illinois University Edwardsville, Edwardsville, IL 62026–1122. Phone: (618) 650–3446; E-mail: ataylor@ siue.edu.

FINAL REFLECTIONS

There is no definitive magic potion to use when creating and maintaining a collaborative teacher research group. Groups are made up of various personalities, and members hold different positions and may play many roles within a group. Also, the research itself will help determine the type and makeup of the group.

To some degree, every group is unique. However, we have learned in this and previous chapters that there are some predictable constants in collaboration (for example, group dynamics) and in teacher research (for example, the process involved). Therefore, we can learn from what others have found to work to strengthen our groups.

Networking and Online Collaborations

This chapter will talk about how collaborative groups work together using networks through online collaboratives or even using school-university partnerships that also exist through networking and via online collaboration tools. Because many of the case examples seemed to fall into this category, the authors and editors felt that networking and online groups were an innovative model of collaborative groups that needed to be discussed. School-university partnerships are quite different from networks, councils, online groups, and so on. School-university partnerships developed more recently through the need for universities to provide professional development for schools. Schools needed the collaborative support of the universities in order to effectively integrate the professional development research and instruction in their schools, ultimately increasing student achievement.

INTRODUCTION

Networking exists by way of collaborative groups that operate as networks or councils, unrelated to particular schools or universities, who work together through networking or online collaborations. This chapter will focus on case studies and effective strategies to allow both groups to collaborate with success. Trends in technology, including increased accessibility of computers for more individuals who can conduct more and more work online, help groups work effectively together. What this chapter is not about is how to work online in areas such as collaborative book productions, or with groups working together in editorial roles, publishing endeavors, or similar situations that utilize online tools to finish products. One particular example you will want to read is the New York State English Council's mission statement for their collaborative group on teacher research, which appears in the Collaboration at Work feature in this chapter. This example provides you with a model on how others are using technology to collaborate effectively.

OVERVIEW OF NETWORKING COMMUNITIES

The author of the poem introducing Part One speaks to communication, stating, "New worlds of thinking evolved from deep conversation." Deep conversations might happen differently depending on the way information is expressed. Collaborative groups within school and online communities use technology to communicate, as the authors of this book can support. The book was constructed entirely through communicating using e-mail, and an occasional phone conference to confirm or refine organization of the book's contents. In fact, as this book was being written, the authors never formerly met. Both authors have similar interests in collaborative relationships and effective teacher education development; the book's conceptual framework extended from their former work on teacher research and ethics of teacher educators. That said, technology is making it easier for research to be conducted, information to be shared, and collaboration to occur. As this chapter was being written, more and more information was published about new and innovative ways to use technology. The *Wall Street Journal* publishes a section called *Technology Journal*. Recent articles in this section speak about blogging as a way to reach new markets, Web-based publications as an alternative to media printing, and search engine tools as a way of offering affordable research alternatives.

As collaborative teacher research groups become the preferred model for conducting research, technology-based resource tools offer attractive alternative methods for publishing research findings, conducting group meetings online, and communicating with other members in a way that increases collaborative effectiveness. Not everyone can participate in collaborative research groups that meet in person regularly. With developments in technology, it becomes increasingly effective to conduct more collaborative tasks online. What types of technological tools are available to your group? Are there professional development topics related to technology that you want to learn about in order to update your knowledge about more current technology resources? What do you think are effective ingredients of online collaborative groups?

This chapter focuses on information technology relative to research collaborative tasks. First, we highlight a discussion on how other collaborative groups use technology. Second, we offer a discussion of innovative methods of technology and strategies to enhance communication and research. Finally, we give a brief overview of how some existing collaborative groups have used technology, along with a discussion of how challenges related to technology are resolved. At this juncture, we will share case studies on effective school-university collaboratives. Before reading this chapter, reflect on how you envision your group's use of technology in order to enhance the research collaborative experience, as well as to achieve the group's overall goals.

Before reading this chapter, consider the following statements:

1. Have you discussed the organizational aspects of using online methods for conducting research and working together?

2. What fears, if any, do you have related to technology integration, or the technical aspects of using online resources as tools to enhance a research collaborative?

3. How will you handle the basic logistics of communicating online? Will you include everyone in all your correspondence? Will your group be selective when sending communications to group members who may or may not be involved?

4. Does your online collaborative have established networking procedures for all members?

5. Have the members discussed compatibility of hardware and software being used by different members?

In previous chapters you learned about four components that influence collaborative relationships and production outcomes and you learned about various types of teacher research collaboratives. Collaborative groups will benefit from reading this chapter because it provides strategies for success that may not have been considered, and gives examples of successful online collaboratives.

As the authors of this book collected information about teacher research collaboratives, the question of how collaboratives integrate technology was asked. One surprising finding was that several of the respondents responded "not applicable" or "none" to this question. This was unexpected, given the many innovative ways technology can be used to enhance the overall collaborative experience. The purpose of the following section is to help groups understand how they can benefit from using technology and not fear to the point that they avoid using it altogether.

ELEMENTS OF EFFECTIVE NETWORKING IN ACTION

Schools that work with universities will need to find ways to effectively document conversations that take place in order to report progress if necessary. One general way to incorporate technology is to record meeting notes and important discussions. This task is generally done by the secretary of the group or the historian. E-mail documents should be explicitly labeled in the subject line so as to track notes at a later date. As groups begin working together and research progress is made, e-mail correspondence becomes the easiest method of recording information and tracking progress. The easiest way to integrate technology is to send notifications or updates about progress through e-mail. The group's decisions about how e-mail will be used and how records are going to be kept should be determined during the organizational meeting.

More and more school-university collaboratives and online networks are turning to public forums to ask questions and garner feedback on their topics. Both authors of this book are members of the National Reading Conference online listserv, which is a way for reading researchers to collaborate with the broader research community. It is not unusual to wake up Monday morning and receive an e-mail from someone on the listserv who needs to find more information about a particular topic. In fact, some groups offer Web sites or make available e-mail addresses for people who read publications by the group, or for those who attend presentations. Using technology as a way to communicate with the public creates community collaboration and allows the groups to understand the public's interest level or support for the topics being investigated. In addition, a Web site or e-mail list will provide a venue for people to submit their ideas relative to the research.

School-university collaborations can also take advantage of using technology when they need access to specific funding sources for their research. Sophisticated search engines make it easier for information to be obtained. Our survey respondents who currently are involved with a research collaborative mentioned obtaining funding to support their research. The U.S. Department of Education maintains an excellent Web site that makes available funding services and grant opportunities for research endeavors. Creating online peer-reviewed journals to provide a venue through which action researchers might share their work or ideas is another way in which technology is being used with research collaborative groups. Online newsletters are another way for groups to disseminate their research findings and communicate with the school community. Two examples of groups who have designed their own Web pages are the following:

- http://pressnetwork.blogspot.com
- teachersnetwork.org

The authors of this book continue to explore online collaboratives and the benefits of research projects done online without meeting. This research has enlightened the many innovative methods in which technology can be used not only with online collaboratives but with all models of research collaboratives at the university, school, or public levels.

Archival Software

An example of one project created by a nonprofit organization is called Dspace Foundation. Dspace offers collaborative groups a place to store research papers and other important documents. Dspace was developed to support collaboration among researchers.

Innovative Funding Opportunities

Collaborative groups trying to obtain funding might consider investigating opportunities with some of the world's biggest technology companies, such as IBM, Apple, Google, and Intel. Recently, IBM awarded grants to several research groups to explore techniques for improving the quality of software, privacy tools, and uses in health care industries.

Guiding Principles for Research Collaboratives

Collaborative groups who want to adopt guiding principles can explore open collaboration research principles, which were created by several universities, technology companies, and the Ewing Marion Kauffman Foundation.

Blogging and Podcasting

With an increase in social networks, collaborative groups have increased opportunities to discuss their research by setting up blogs or podcasts. Tools that can be used to create blog space are Web 2.0 tools. Video podcast sites such as YouTube are another way for researchers to share ideas.

Collaborative Foundations

Foundations are being formed that support research collaboratives. For example, the following offer a place for ideas to be communicated and discussed:

- John S. and James L. Knight Foundation's Idealab
  http://idealab.com
- John D. and Catherine T. MacArthur Foundation's Spotlight Blog
  http://spotlight.macfound.org

The possibilities for innovative technology integration are endless and by the time this volume is published, updated versions and models will already be published and used. As new technologies are being used a greater emphasis on professional development for collaborative groups will be necessary. No longer is it effective to report that technology integration is not being used or not applicable, because there are too many effective ways in which technology should and can be used.

NETWORKING GROUPS

The Internet has made it not only feasible but easy to network with teacher researchers from around the world. We also network with colleagues when we attend professional conferences and workshops. Networking is a dynamic means of communicating with colleagues with similar interests, sharing knowledge and resources, and opening conversations up to potential collaboration. Networking is the idea of having professional connections with others, either face-to-face or online (see Chapter Five) or other means of communication. Network participants usually support each other in a distant way that might lead to collaboration. Think of networks as external support groups that help you achieve your goals. These colleagues might not be working in your classroom helping you collect data, but they may be able to provide leads for analyzing or interpreting your data by recommending resources. Chapter Ten shares in-depth information about a very prominent teacher research network, the Fairfax County Public Schools Teacher Researcher Network. Here are several examples of other well-developed networks.

Rebecca Rogers wrote to us about her networked group, which is called the Literacy for Social Justice Teacher Research Group. She and Mary Ann Kramer cofounded the group to network a community of educators in the St. Louis area who are committed to teaching for social justice. Rebecca attributes the success of her group to the fact that it has what she calls a "participatory design." That is, the group is constantly evolving to meet the needs of its members. The group has a summer institute, which provides time to rejuvenate, reflect on past accomplishments, and plan for the upcoming year. There are about 150 members on the group's listserv, through which they network to support each other, to share information and resources, and to discuss relevant ideas. The group is also featured in Chapter Three's Collaboration at Work. For more information about the group and to join, visit its Web site at www.umsl.edu/~lsjtrg.

The American Educational Research Association's Action Research Special Interest Group is an international network for teacher researchers.

Their purpose is to "involve teachers, administrators, researchers, and community members in dialogue about action research that examines educational practice and encourages educational reform and professional development" (http://aera.net/default.aspx?menu_id=26&id=973).

The Teachers Network Leadership Institute at www.teachersnetwork.org was created to improve students' learning by bringing teachers' voices to educational policymaking through the dissemination of action research findings. The action research studies designed by the Institute's Fellows address the link between policymaking and student achievement.

Finally, the New York State English Council supports a teacher inquiry initiative. This state affiliate of the National Council of Teachers of English sponsors a teacher research blog, promotes the publication of teacher research in its journal, offers minigrants, and highlights teacher research as a strand in their annual conference in the state's capital. It is currently expanding a mentorship network throughout the state to provide consultative support for teacher researchers. This group is featured in Collaboration at Work in this chapter.

These types of collaborative groups go beyond colleagues working on a research project together. Networks provide a forum for professional development that allows us to "rub virtual elbows with colleagues" (Vascellero, 2007, p. 1). They are a means of commiserating with people with similar interests and, perhaps, different backgrounds and experiences, so we can learn from many.

COLLABORATION AT WORK

The New York State English Council
Contributed by Tim Fredrick

When the New York State English Council (NYSEC) formed the Standing Committee for Teacher Inquiry, its primary goal was to promote teacher research among elementary and secondary teachers so their voices could be heard in their schools, districts, and the state education department. Our mission statement follows:

> *The New York State English Council has formed the Standing Committee on Teacher Inquiry to support ELA teachers of all levels across the state in conducting teacher inquiry studies in their classrooms and in disseminating this research to a wider audience. The committee seeks to provide classroom teachers with the resources necessary to conduct teacher inquiry studies that can serve as effective professional development, as a strategy for increasing student achievement, and as a productive means for educational policy advocacy.*

The committee offers support to teacher researchers through resource recommendations, research mentoring, networking, funding, and dissemination opportunities. These systems of support aim to facilitate the growth of teacher research, which will promote lasting changes in teaching and learning across schools, districts, and the state for years to come.

The committee has worked to develop a network of research mentors, experienced teacher researchers, who are prepared to help teacher teams in person or via phone and the Internet. Some of these groups are university-school partnerships; other groups are happening within K–12 schools among colleagues. This ongoing mentoring network provides the type of capacity building that will last for years at a school site as research teams guide new teachers through the inquiry process.

NYSEC offers opportunities for teacher researchers to share and publicize their findings. Dissemination of research results is key to helping teams advocate on the building, district, and state levels. In addition to a monthly feature column about teacher inquiry, NYSEC's award-winning journal *The English Record* is committed to publishing solid articles describing teacher research studies. Also, NYSEC has been working with the State Department of Education to disseminate findings through a statewide *E-Blast* that is regularly e-mailed to districts across the state to provide up-to-date resources and information on the English language arts. NYSEC also invites teacher researchers to present their findings at its annual conference. A special

Teacher Inquiry Strand brings researchers and teachers together to provide peer-to-peer support. Finally, the committee provides training with new Internet technologies, such as blogs and wikis, to easily disseminate findings. Teachers who take on the responsibility of studying teacher and strategy effectiveness cannot and should not be abandoned in this process. They need support and resources to make the changes they envision become reality. The New York English Council's Standing Committee of Teacher Inquiry facilitates and supports teacher research projects through statewide collaboration.

IMPACT OF NETWORKING PARTNERSHIPS IN COLLABORATION

The impact that school-based collaboratives have on communities extends beyond technology integration. The way in which groups communicate the process of their research is leading them to develop Web sites as a way to disseminate and involve the broader public in their thinking. One mature collaborative group has developed an innovative Web site as a way to communicate research. Their success in using technology is recorded in a statement below:

Our website and listserv have been essential in organizing our group. We send out email reminders of our next meetings, important events around the area, leadership, advocacy and teaching opportunities. Our website also posts our upcoming meetings but it also includes a description of other aspects of our group which has been very helpful in orienting new members to the group. In terms of technology during our meetings, this has been a challenge because where we often meet does not have updated technology (it is an adult education site with a leaky roof and they have threatened to close the building several times!). We often struggle to play a PowerPoint presentation because sometimes the technology works and sometimes it does not. The center does not have a DVD player either which makes viewing newer DVDs a challenge. WE often play them off of a computer.

—Dr. Rebecca Rogers, University of Missouri–St. Louis; Mary Ann Kramer, literacy coordinator for St. Louis Public Schools Adult Education

LSJTRG was highlighted in an article in *Rethinking Schools* focused on teacher groups committed to social justice. The article was called "Teacher Organizers Take Quality into Their Own Hands" (2005–2006, Volume 20, 2). LSJTRG was included in a book called *Educators on the Frontline: Advocacy Strategies for Your Classroom, Your School, Your Profession* (2005, International Reading Association).

Recently I put together the *Handbook of Research on Reading Comprehension* with my coeditor, Gerry G. Duffy. What we thought would be a daunting task turned out to be a positive online collaborative with more than thirty literacy professionals who helped author chapters, make recommendations to research, and meet critical deadlines to get the book completed on deadline. What made this experience successful was that when Gerry and I met at the IRA conference in Chicago to discuss the planning of the handbook, we also discussed the following:

1. Policies and procedures of dealing with authors

2. Roles of each editor

3. Responses to contributors' writing needs, such as ability to meet deadlines or ability to locate content area research

4. Deadlines for editors and authors

5. Personal annoyances and how we would handle them (Gerry was very flexible!)

Much of what we discussed in our first meeting, prior to completing the entire handbook via online collaboration, were strategies that we thought would make our work successful. Communication was key to our success with the contributors. We maintained a supportive research community and ensured the contributors that we would be happy to work with them but also made our expectations very clear. Gerry and I worked together to establish procedures for the contributors and we maintained our editorial roles. As first editor, Gerry respected my ability to provide the organization structure. In return, I relied on Gerry to oversee the project with a critical literacy lens. One e-mail speaks to this:

> Hi Susan—Thanks for the offer to help but there's not much to do—just wait for the finished chapters to arrive. If you've had a chance to revise the front matter, I'd like to look at that . . . In addition, we have to talk about the lack of landmark studies (as you pointed out) and what counts as evidence (the tension a contributor points out in her chapter). Anything else that occurs to you? (Personal e-mail communication, May 2, 2007)

In summary, the keys to our online collaborative success can be attributed to the following elements:

- Positive communication
- Constructive support
- Productive goals established
- Practical working standards that meet the needs of both editors
- Creative use of new ideas

REFLECTING ON NETWORKING PARTNERSHIPS IN COLLABORATION

With the writing of this book in its final stages, we authors have worked together but have yet to meet each other face-to-face. This is our third publication together. The first two are *Teachers Taking Action* (2008), published by the International Reading Association, and *The Ethical Educator* (2007), published by Peter Lang. All of our work has been done online. We have created a network of teacher researchers who also enjoy writing and publishing. We believe our relationship as online colleagues can inspire other researchers to value technology as a resource to bridge research communities.

Our online collaborative success might be evaluated by a similar set of work ethics, respect for deadlines, and communication that focuses primarily on positive actions and results. We enjoy each other's openness to new ideas and are respectful of each other's time when external deadlines need attention and our research needs to wait a bit. We like writing and research because we value making a contribution to teachers and researchers. Similar values are based in the knowledge that our work is done out of love.

Our work is not done out of a desire for professional growth for oneself and not the other. We work together. We are forgiving if something was not communicated clearly. We are willing to explore new ideas at the risk of not producing positive results. We are not afraid to question each other's decisions when appropriate. We accept and respect established roles.

What teachers and researchers can learn from this chapter is that online collaboratives can be a positive tool that can promote research. Next, you will read about a districtwide model collaborative group that has developed into an extremely successful action research community.

A Districtwide Model

The Fairfax County Public Schools Teacher Researcher Network

Contributed by Gail V. Ritchie

How to Use This Chapter

In this chapter, I will share my experiences with the Fairfax County Public Schools Teacher Researcher Network to provide the reader with information about an established and thriving collaborative teacher research community. This chapter will inform you of the value of collaborative teacher research as an ideal means of ongoing, job-embedded professional development.

FOUNDING THE NETWORK

Perhaps it is not just coincidental that Fairfax County Public Schools is one of the best-performing districts in the nation and that teacher research has been going on in Fairfax County since 1979. The Fairfax County Public Schools Teacher Researcher Network, in its current form, was first established as the Teacher Researcher Project in the mid-1990s through a grant from the U.S. Department of Education. Drawing upon their fifteen years of experience leading teacher research, in their grant proposal, Marian Mohr, Mary Ann Nocerino, and Courtney Rogers—whom we endearingly refer to as the "founding mothers"—recommended establishing a network that would feature support for teacher researchers in the form of

- Experienced teacher researcher leaders
- Opportunities for collaboration
- Time to meet
- Support for writing and publishing
- Public recognition of teacher research
- Support of building administrators (Mohr, Rogers, Sanford, Nocerino, MacLean, & Clawson, 2004, pp. 4–5)

Further details about the grant and the initial formation of the network can be found in the book *Teacher Research for Better Schools* (Mohr, Rogers, Sanford, Nocerino, MacLean, & Clawson, 2004).

ORGANIZING THE NETWORK

After almost thirty years in existence, research in Fairfax County Public Schools has flexible but enduring procedures for establishing and supporting teacher research groups. The mission of the FCPS Teacher Researcher Network is to provide support for practicing teacher researchers and education to others about the work of teacher researchers. In support of this mission, the school district's Department of Professional Learning and Training (PLT) provides three days of release time per teacher researcher by funding payment for substitute teachers. PLT also provides a stipend for teacher research group leaders, in recognition of their expertise and the time commitment involved in leading their groups.

The FCPS Network is open to any teacher, administrator, curriculum specialist, or school counselor who is interested in improving his or her practice through reflection and inquiry. Usually, a teacher or group of teachers will form a teacher research group at their school, and then that group will officially join the network by submitting a list of their names to the network coleaders. This kind of accountability is necessary in order to accurately budget for the funding of substitute teachers.

Once a group is formed at a school, the group identifies a leader or coleaders and schedules a series of meetings that will take them through the school year as well as through the teacher research process from casting questions all the way through sharing conclusions and implications. It is up to each group how often the meetings take place, but typically the groups meet for six half-days between October and April, as that enables them to make full use of the school district funding.

The network coleaders communicate with group leaders via an e-mail distribution list. We maintain an online Blackboard site, which contains documents and resources helpful to teacher researchers. We also have a public Web site, which informs others about the existence and work of the Network: www.fcps.edu/plt/tresearch.htm.

At the beginning of each school year, the coleaders of the Network invite all current and former members of the Network to attend a kick-off session in late September. At this session, attendees share their research interests, discuss the similarities and differences between "research" and "teacher research," assist one another in casting questions, and experience firsthand the process and benefits of writing in a reflective journal. An invitation to join the Network is also sent to all FCPS employees by posting an item in the school division's biweekly electronic newsletter.

Every participant in the Network is considered a teacher researcher. A school-based reading teacher and I, a K–6 instructional coach, are the current coleaders of the Network. There is also a resource teacher working in the Department of Professional Learning and Training who oversees the bureaucratic aspects of keeping the Network functioning. For us, it is important to keep a close connection to the school's point of view, so at least one coleader is always a school-based person. What this means is that teacher research is not a top-down initiative in our district; instead, it was a grassroots initiative that has grown into a district-supported network that is committed to supporting teacher research at the school and classroom level.

Each of the teacher research groups, most of which are school-based, meets regularly during the school year. Many of the groups follow an outline based on tentative research plans and a timetable. (See Exhibit 10.1.) Following this series of prompts for reflection and discussion takes researchers through the teacher research process from casting a question, collecting and analyzing data, forming conclusions, and through to considering implications of their findings.

Exhibit 10.1: Tentative Research Plans and Timetable

SEPTEMBER—BEGIN A RESEARCH LOG. DISCUSS AND REFLECT ON THE FOLLOWING:

What is research?

What is teacher research?

How do I find out about what interests me?

What are the expectations for this project?

How does one develop teacher research questions?

How do I find my research questions?

What is my research question?

OCTOBER—BEGIN THE DATA COLLECTION

How do I find out more about what interests me?

How am I looking at what I am curious about?

What is data?

What does it tell me?

How can I begin collecting data?

How do I revise my research question?

NOVEMBER—CONTINUE AND EXPAND METHODS OF DATA COLLECTION

What data is emerging?

Where does the data lead me?

What else do I want to know?

How else can I be collecting data?

(continued)

(continued)

DECEMBER—BEGIN THE ANALYSIS

What questions are emerging from the data?

What is my research question now?

What does the data mean?

JANUARY—COMPLETE MAJOR DATA COLLECTION

Looking at data as a whole, what is my research question?

What do I think I have learned so far?

FEBRUARY—WRAP UP DATA COLLECTION AND BEGIN DRAFT WRITING

MARCH—FOCUS ON YOUR DRAFT WRITING

What am I learning?

How can I best show what I have learned?

Are there gaps in my research?

APRIL—NARROW YOUR FOCUS

What are my findings?

What are the implications for further study or action?

MAY—DEADLINE DRAFT DUE

Share your draft with others—perhaps roundtable discussions with school faculty

SUMMER—REVISE AND PREPARE FOR POSSIBLE PUBLICATION

Source: Excerpted, with permission from the National Writing Project, from Marion S. MacLean and Marian M. Mohr, 2007, *Teacher-Researchers at Work*. Berkeley, CA: National Writing Project, pp. 25–26. Copyright © 1999 National Writing Project.

Leaders who are new to teacher research, new to leading a research group, or both, meet six times per year to work with our teacher research consultants. These consultants are two other "founding mothers": Courtney Rogers and Mary Ann Nocerino. At these meetings, which we call Teacher Research Group Leader Forums, group leaders learn how to facilitate the research of others at the same time that they are learning new strategies and ideas to further their own inquiries. Based on their many years of experience supporting teacher research, for the upcoming school year, Rogers and Nocerino have planned the topics shown in Table 10.1.

Recognizing that experienced group leaders would also appreciate the opportunity to meet periodically, we have planned a separate series of meetings for them in which they will be able

TABLE 10.1. *Planning Discussion Topics in Advance*

Defining teacher research and getting started

Identifying and responding to research questions

Beginning a research log and collecting data

Examining assumptions, beliefs, and biases

Revising research questions

Sharing and responding to data

Fitting questions to data

Data validation and how teacher researchers can help each other

Establishing ethics and standards for teacher research

Data analysis, Part I: Strategies for reviewing and analyzing data

Data analysis, Part II: Looking at data as a whole and moving from data analysis to findings and implications

Writing about research

Sharing findings and implications

FCPS database

to network with each other, strengthen collegial relationships, expand their knowledge of the process of teacher research, and refine their leadership and facilitative capabilities. Proposed topics for these meetings include those in Table 10.2.

The meetings for new leaders and for experienced leaders are three hours in length and are highly interactive. Usually the meetings take place in the afternoons, with light refreshments provided. Examples of some of the experiences in which attendees engage include:

TABLE 10.2. *Proposed Topics*

Beginning the year

Advertising your group

Inviting members

Casting a question

Sharing

Data collection

Data analysis

Writing about research

Ideas for sharing findings

- Discussions of terms such as *research*
- Responding to prompting questions by talking at tables and sharing out with the whole group
- Reading and discussing short excerpts related to the teacher research process
- Carousel brainstorming, in which attendees write down ideas or plans on pieces of chart paper, then rotate around the room commenting upon each other's ideas
- Writing in reflective journals

Some of our researchers also apply to participate as fellows in the Teachers Network Leadership Institute (TNLI) (www.teachersnetwork.org/tnli/index.htm). TNLI was founded as part of the work of Teachers Network, and its goal is to promote the inclusion of teachers' knowledge in policy decision making. Each year, the Fairfax County Public Schools affiliate of TNLI pays a stipend of $1,000 to ten fellows, who are selected based on their commitment to studying the policy implications of their research. TNLI provides teachers with opportunities to further develop their knowledge and skills to conduct teacher research and to use the research findings to influence policy at the local, state, and national levels. TNLI Fellows' work includes: framing practical policy positions that relate to improved student achievement; engaging the public and elected officials in community conversations about education; participating on advisory boards, panels, and task forces; and publishing or disseminating findings and recommendations nationwide. The FCPS TNLI fellows engage in face-to-face meetings and online discussions to support one another's inquiries. Planned topics for discussion during the 2007–08 school year include those in Table 10.3.

TABLE 10.3. *Topics for the 2007–08 School Year*

Meeting Focus
Beginning the year
Casting a question
Refining the question
Determining what data will help answer the question
Discussing: What is policy?
Data collection
Data analysis
Policy levels
Writing about research
Ideas for sharing findings
Findings and policy implications
17th annual conference

During the 2006–07 school year, the Network supported the research efforts of 223 teacher researchers in twenty-five school-based groups and one countywide group of technology specialists. At the beginning of the 2007–08 school year, thirty-three schools had joined the Network. By midyear, that number had grown to thirty-five groups.

To support its goal of providing support for the sharing of teacher research findings, for the past sixteen years the Teacher Researcher Network has also cosponsored, and now solely sponsors, an Annual Teacher Researcher Conference. At the most recent conference, the more than 250 attendees enjoyed an evening of learning, sharing, and discussing how teacher research increases student learning across departments, grade levels, and disciplines, as well as how teacher research increases dialogue, collaboration, and sharing of instructional issues. The conference featured poster exhibits, roundtable discussions, and interactive workshops by teacher researchers and administrators.

The conference included teacher leaders and administrators from across all grade levels and from several school districts in the Washington, DC, metropolitan area. The research topics were varied, showcasing a wide range of disciplines and student populations. Conference attendees were able to network with like-minded colleagues to learn about and discuss such topics as:

- Narrowing the Student Achievement Gap with Teacher Research in Mathematics
- Building a Buzz About Books with a Blog
- Lesson Study
- Using Primary Resources
- How Parent Centers Impact Elementary School Communities
- Using the SmartBoard for Effective Instruction Across the Curriculum
- User-Friendly Independent Studies for Gifted Middle School Students

THE FOCUS FOR THE NETWORK

Because Fairfax County Public Schools is a very large school district, we do not have a division-wide theme for teacher research. Rather, we ask teacher researchers to consider the school board's vision that "Fairfax County Public Schools, a world-class school system, inspires, enables, and empowers students to meet high academic standards, lead ethical lives, and demonstrate responsible citizenship" (FCPS, 2007). Within this vision, the school board has articulated specific goals:

- All students will obtain, understand, analyze, communicate, and apply knowledge and skills to achieve success in school and in life.
- All students will demonstrate the aptitude, attitude, and skills to lead responsible, fulfilling, and respectful lives.
- All students will understand and model the important attributes that people must have to contribute to an effective and productive community and the common good of all.

Further information about these goals can be found at www.fcps.edu/schlbd/sg/goals.htm.

Within these three broad goals, individual teacher researchers, or teams of teacher researchers, identify question or "puzzlements" (Jacob, 2000, p. 12) related to their own contexts. This then forms the basis of their inquiries. Through participation in their school groups, teacher researchers refine their questions, collect data to help them answer their questions, analyze the data, and draw conclusions based on that analysis. Teacher research in Fairfax County Public Schools is a powerful vehicle for teachers to study their own practice and its impact on student achievement in relation to the school board goals.

STRENGTHS AND CHALLENGES

A major strength of the FCPS Teacher Researcher Network is its continuity. Throughout its long history, our Network has remained true to its mission of supporting the work of teacher researchers while educating others about the work of teacher researchers. Several of the "founding mothers" are still active in the Network, as evidenced by Mary Ann Nocerino's and Courtney Rogers's consultancy work with teacher research group leaders. At most of the school sites, sustainability is built into the group structure. For example, when I left my original school group for a two-year stint at PLT, two of my colleagues took over the leadership of the group. When one of them moved to another school, a third colleague took over her position. Another thing that keeps the Network strong is the tendency of teacher researchers to start up a new group when they move to a new school. One of our current group leaders has led three groups at three different schools. Finally, group leaders are always willing to mentor colleagues who are new to leading a group. I myself benefited from such mentorship and in turn provided it to several others. Exhibit 10.2, begun by Marian Mohr, and added to over the years, highlights major events in the history of our network.

EXHIBIT 10.2: MAJOR EVENTS IN THE HISTORY OF THE FCPS TEACHER RESEARCHER NETWORK

1979–1982

- First teacher research group forms. Supported by Northern Virginia Writing Project.
- Teacher Research Seminar first offered by Fairfax County Public Schools (FCPS) and George Mason University.

1982–1986

- First school-based teacher research groups at Langston Hughes Middle School. Similar groups formed at Falls Church and West Potomac High Schools.
- Elementary school research groups formed to study new language arts curriculum.
- FCPS teacher researchers publish in professional journals and books.

1986–1991

- More teacher research groups formed with FCPS teacher researchers continuing to publish and give presentations at local, state, and national conferences.
- First Northern Virginia Teacher Researcher Conference sponsored by FCPS, the Northern Virginia Writing Project, and the Greater Washington Reading Council.

- Two FCPS teacher researchers publish *Working Together: A Guide for Teacher Researchers* (National Council of Teachers of English).

1991–1994

- Teacher research made part of many local masters and doctoral programs with enrollment by many FCPS teachers.
- FCPS teacher researchers receive grants available through IMPACT II and other local, state, and national professional organizations.

1994–1997

- The Teacher Researcher Project, funded by an Office of Educational Research and Improvement (OERI) grant supports school-based teacher research groups at Lemon Road ES, Poe MS, and Falls Church HS.
- Teacher research leadership and reflective practice courses offered as part of FCPS Academy Courses.
- Teacher research leaders from approximately twenty-five schools organize to form the FCPS Teacher Researcher Network. Initiate teacher research database and newsletter.
- FCPS teacher researchers give presentations at the International Conference of Teacher Research, American Educational Research Association, National Staff Development Council, and Association for Supervision and Curriculum Development.
- Teacher Research Network sponsors workshops for teachers, administrators, and families.

1997–2008

- Two FCPS teacher researchers publish *Teacher Researchers at Work* (National Writing Project).
- Spencer Foundation awards grant to support writing of research related to three-year study of teacher research in schools. Results appear in the publication of *Teacher Research for Better Schools* (Teachers College Press) by six FCPS teacher researchers.
- Teacher research groups contribute to school planning, evaluation, and improvement.
- Teacher research in FCPS is now supported by a Blackboard site.
- FCPS teacher researchers are leaders in national networks of the American Educational Association and the National Staff Development Council.
- An FCPS teacher researcher receives Cyber Education Champion Award, a national award from the Business Software Alliance, for her commitment to teaching students and educators about cyber ethics.
- The FCPS Teacher Research Network joins with the Association of Teacher Educators (ATE) to hold a two-day conference, highlighting the importance of teacher research and the university-teacher partnership.
- An FCPS teacher conducts a dissertation study entitled *Teacher Research as a Habit of Mind*, designed to investigate the research question: "What are the essential elements for engaging and sustaining teachers in teacher research?"

Another major strength is the strong model we've established for facilitating teacher research. In my dissertation study (Ritchie, 2006), I found that the quality of a group leader's facilitation is a major factor in whether or not teachers continue as researchers from year to year. Study participants from an international teacher research network, a national teacher research network, and a school district's teacher research network identified qualities and categories of support that were necessary in an effective research facilitator. See Tables 10.4 through 10.6.

This information affirms the importance and value of FCPS Network's use of ongoing professional development for our novice group leaders. Through these meetings, the Network helps leaders who are continuing to learn the process of teacher research while building their capacities for leadership and facilitation. Additionally, responding to requests to provide a forum for continuing professional development for experienced group leaders, we have added a series of meetings for them as well. These meetings are designed for experienced group leaders who want to network with each other, strengthen collegial relationships, expand their knowledge of the process of teacher research, and refine their leadership and facilitative capabilities.

TABLE 10.4. *The International Network*

Personal Qualities	Organizational Actions	Research Process Actions
Provides emotional support	Provide funds	Know how to access necessary resources
Responsive	Provide technology	Ask questions
Inspiring	Schedule regular meetings	Invite questions
Enthusiastic	Facilitate	Provide alternative viewpoints
Engaged	Create opportunities for collaboration and discussion	Model, guide, support, and sustain research process
Encouraging	Take notes and distribute to all group members	Obtain release time
Motivating	Ensure consistent contact	Share teacher research
An active listener	Provide feedback	Connect to other teacher researchers (local, regional, national, and international)
		Sustain focus
		Stress importance of gathering data
		Help with data analysis
		Help with writing
		Provide a safe place to experiment and try out new ideas
		Conduct mini in-service information sessions

Source: Ritchie, 2006, pp. 192–194.

TABLE 10.5. *The National Network*

Personal Qualities	Organizational Actions	Research Process Actions
Encouraging	Encourage discourse	Teach the process
Provides moral support	Build community; allow time for friendship, bonding, and sharing	Help define the term *teacher research*
Motivating	Use flexible grouping to work with teachers (one-to-one, research buddy/ partner, small group)	Help with research
Open and flexible	Build capacity by recognizing and training other potential group leaders	Help clarify questions
Provides ongoing support and assistance	Give feedback, input, and suggestions	Share own discoveries
	Provide "just-in-time" support	Read, question, and suggest ways to look at data, people to talk with, and literature to read
	Provide time for troubleshooting and collaboration	Realize that teacher research does not always have to be formal
	Make time to meet with the researchers	Help teachers select and explore areas of interest
	Facilitate meetings	Provide different models of how teacher research can be conducted
	Provide materials (such as notebook, handouts, log book)	Act as a resource
	Promote formal and informal conversations	Help with writing
		Provide a timetable and checkpoints

Source: Ritchie, 2006, pp. 192–194.

TABLE 10.6. *The Local Network*

Personal Qualities	Organizational Actions	Research Process Actions
Encouraging	Check in	Point out other research
Motivating	Provide feedback	Structure meetings to include time for writing, discussion, viewing, and analyzing data
Open-minded	Provide a nurturing environment and a learning community	Model reflective practice

(continued)

TABLE 10.6. *The Local Network (continued)*

Personal Qualities	Organizational Actions	Research Process Actions
Collaborative	Positive reinforcement	Ask questions
An active listener	Coordinate time to meet and share	Answer questions
Accessible	Supply resources and materials	Make suggestions
Consistent	Act as a mediator to administration	Guide participants in the research process
Celebrates what has been learned	Facilitate and guide	Help to streamline research questions
	Look for funding	Infuse ideas; brainstorm
	Provide time for exchange of ideas	Assist with data analysis
	Follow up one-on-one outside of meetings	Model the process of gathering and analyzing data
	Maintain regular contact	Educate
	Discuss what has been learned with educational community (students, families, other educators)	Make research part of the school culture; focus on issues unique to the particular school
	Provide concrete advice	Keep members on track
		Set deadlines
		Share successful processes; lead by example
		Encourage researchers to examine assumptions
		Involve educational community in the process
		Help refocus

Source: Ritchie, 2006, pp. 192–194.

A major challenge to the continued existence and vibrancy of the Network is money. It is very costly to fund the release time for every teacher researcher and the stipends for the group leaders. A second challenge is that some administrators are reluctant to have their teacher researchers meet during school hours. So far, I have been successful in arguing that the budget is justified because teacher research is a very cost-effective means of providing job-embedded, ongoing professional learning—the "gold standard" for professional development as advocated by the National Staff Development Council (NSDC, 2007). For reluctant administrators, I have used the argument that teachers who conduct research actually get better at teaching, which is a "win" situation for students and for the school.

As coleader of the FCPS Network, I don't have any authority over building-level decisions. If an administrator decides not to support teacher research, there is little I can do about it at that school. I have made personal appeals, and in some instances, persuaded a reluctant administrator to "have a go" with teacher research in his or her building. In other cases, I have encouraged teachers to join a teacher research group at a nearby school. Some have done that.

METHODOLOGICAL CONSIDERATIONS

The most helpful resources and tools in the collaborative work of the FCPS Teacher Researcher Network have been the veteran teacher researchers and the books written by the "founding mothers" (MacLean & Mohr, 1999; Mohr et al., 2004). Another important factor in the collaborative work of teacher researchers at individual school sites is a supportive context for their inquiries. In my dissertation study (Ritchie, 2006), I found that the type of environment needed for teacher research is one that is built on mutual responsibility and trust, collaboration, focus on student learning, as well as creating and generating knowledge about praxis. Engaging and sustaining teachers in teacher research requires a shift in culture from teachers working in isolation to teachers working collaboratively. Schools that have adopted the philosophy and practices of professional learning communities are ideal contexts for teacher research. Through inquiry, teachers can generate knowledge about best practice, develop efficacy and a sense of agency, and find their voices. Ideally, we would provide this collaborative inquiry opportunity to a larger percentage of the school division's more than eleven thousand teachers, but that would require much greater amounts of money.

IMPACT OF THE NETWORK

There are many indicators that the work of the Network's teacher researchers has influenced teaching and learning. The most recent Teacher Researcher Conference had over 250 attendees, including a teacher from Minneapolis, Minnesota, and a university-level educator from West Chester, Pennsylvania. These educators attended because they wanted to learn more about the FCPS Network in order to support teacher research in their own contexts. Rising student scores are a source of "hard" data regarding the positive impact of teacher research, but we also have data from the teachers themselves. Through their informal sharing during teacher research group meetings, their roundtable discussions at our annual conference, and the project summaries posted on our teacher leadership database (accessible only to FCPS employees), teacher researchers speak eloquently of the positive effect that engaging in inquiry has had on their educational knowledge and instructional practices. The information presented below is drawn from the historical documents of the FCPS Teacher Researcher Network.

Fairfax County teacher researchers participate in school-based professional learning and travel to nearby schools to give presentations about teacher research and to support teacher research groups. They are invited speakers at conferences nationwide, where and when time and finances permit. FCPS teacher researchers represent our school district at state and national conferences of such organizations as the International Conference of Teacher Research (ICTR), National Staff Development Council (NSDC), the Association of Supervision and Curriculum Development (ASCD), the American Educational Research Association (AERA), and conferences related to specific disciplines such as the National Council of Teachers of Mathematics, the International Reading Association, and the National Council of Teachers of English. FCPS teacher researchers lead the special interest group of NSDC in Teacher Research and are active members of the Teacher Research special interest group within the American Educational Research Association.

FCPS teacher researchers have received teacher researcher grants through the Greater Washington Reading Council, the Virginia State Reading Association, the International Reading Association, the National Council of Teachers of English, IMPACT II, the Spencer Foundation, the National Education Association, the Virginia Education Association, the Fairfax Education Association, *The Washington Post,* and the Office of Educational Research.

Teacher research groups form a professional learning community within a school and foster a collegial exchange of ideas focused on student learning and student achievement. Experienced teacher researchers give presentations to and with their colleagues. Because of their knowledge about teaching and learning specific to their schools, teacher researchers offer data-based decision making and, when possible, participate in school planning, evaluation, and governance. When test scores, targets, and school plans focus on a school's efforts at improvement, teachers' research offers information about *why* and *how* teaching and learning could change in an effort to improve instruction and student achievement.

When students know about and participate in their teacher's research, they, too, analyze their own learning. They acquire many different ways to learn. There is increasing evidence that students who know how they learn and who have more than one strategy for solving problems are more successful learners and test takers than those who have only a single strategy for approaching a learning task. Within the context of teacher research, student differences are recognized and valued, high expectations of achievement are individualized, and students learn from each other.

The preceding history of our Network was originally written by Marian Mohr, then modified by Network coleaders Carleen Payne, Denny Berry, and now by me. This ongoing, collaborative effort exemplifies how our Network evolves yet remains connected to its history.

FUTURE DIRECTIONS

We hope to grow the Network from its current thirty-five groups to fifty or more groups within the next five years. To do this, we will continue to "spread the joy" about the purpose and value of teacher research to as many people as possible. I will also continue my quest to help teachers bring their voices to the policy arena and share the findings and implications from their teacher research studies.

LESSONS LEARNED

Through my membership in the FCPS Teacher Researcher Network, and through my work as coleader for the past two years, I have gained a deeper appreciation for the value of inquiry supported by collaboration. Thoughtful, reflective educators who seek to answer classroom questions through their inquiries join together to share their questions, successes, and findings. We all—teachers, students, administrators—benefit from the knowledge generated by this ongoing professional dialogue. Through funding and a supportive organizational structure, the Network supports teacher research as a way of being, rather than an add-on to already overburdened teaching lives.

THINKING TOGETHER: CREATING AND SUSTAINING PROFESSIONAL LEARNING COMMUNITIES

Contributed by Ginny Goatley

In this chapter, I recognized many parallels with my own experiences in professional learning communities. In fact, I went back to an article from 1994 that I wrote with a group of colleagues about our Teacher Research Group (see Goatley et al., 1994). Two primary benefits of our association in the group included a sense of professionalism and the development of a community involving sharing, nurturing, and learning. As educators, it is critically important for us to have communities to share our ideas, extend our knowledge, and pursue professional aspects of our careers.

Since my experience with this Teacher Research Group in the early 1990s I have been fortunate to work with several other professional learning communities for teachers. In this process, I learned a number of key processes that help to start and maintain such communities.

1. *Common goals.* It is useful to have common goals for the purpose and intent of the gatherings. At the same time, a group that has diversity of ideas and intent is also useful for provoking extending conversations that "challenge the known" and move people to consider ideas they had not previously considered. Explicit discussions about what the group wants to accomplish and how they might go about reaching that goal is an essential beginning for any group. Of course, negotiating those goals and making useful changes will help the group continue to prosper and extend the longevity of the collaboration.

2. *Professional atmosphere.* As educators, we want to have opportunities to engage in professional conversations about our teaching. Teacher research group meetings provide such an atmosphere. It is useful for the group to have an agenda or a routine format, such as taking turns on who is presenting their work, focusing on a particular issue, or reading an article to discuss. Then people are prepared for the conversation and it becomes more productive. Of course, any gathering should also have time for pressing concerns that developed since the previous meeting.

3. *Setting.* We are busy people with many aspects to our lives! Many of my colleagues participate in groups because they get so much out of them in terms of professional growth, knowledge, and affirmation. Picking a setting that is convenient for the majority of the group and meeting at a regular time are most conducive to keeping the group together. Teachers in school districts that have this time built into the school day are quite fortunate to have such a forward-looking administration. However, not all teachers are in such schools, and these individuals may be looking to collaborate with educators from other schools who have similar interests. Once there is an established group, try to keep to a routine for group meetings. A setting that involves a meal or some type of food seems to have a bonding effect!

4. *What do we call ourselves?* Though "Teacher Research Group" seems to be a prominent title for groups of teachers interested in pursuing research in their classrooms, I've seen a range of titles and goals for such professional learning communities. In some cases, teachers have strongly argued against the word *research* as not really representing the reflective and action-oriented goals of their particular group. In the end, many outsiders might recognize

(continued)

(continued)

the work they do as teacher research, but it is critical for the group to define their own goals and purpose, including how they refer to themselves (see Richardson, 1994, for various definitions). It can sometimes be the case that teachers start a group for their own internal reasons, thinking the goal is simply to inform what happens in their own classrooms, and only later come to appreciate how their research might inform audiences beyond their classrooms and school districts.

5. *Knowing when to start and when to end.* Teachers participate in research for their own goals and purposes as well as to be part of a broader professional community. In my book club with a group of friends, participants come and go based on their schedules, interests, and life circumstances, yet a solid core of people has continued for many years. I've had similar experiences with teacher research groups. It may be that a group starts for a particular reason, such as having received a grant, and then disbands when the grant ends or the group leader moves on to another project. In other groups, the members have been meeting for years with changes based on their interests and goals for a new project. Certainly, I've found that the key to increasing the longevity of a group is to keep it flexible and include time for discussion of "How is it going?" and "What do we want to change, if anything, about how we engage in conversation?" Just as we need to be considerate of how our groups are formed and change as the group learns, I think we need to understand how our groups might end. It is fine for a group to finalize a project and stop meeting, as that does not necessarily end the professional learning. It is simply a step toward the next project, which might then be reconfigured to include new members interested in a particular topic. Plus, I find great pleasure in catching up with friends from earlier groups and learning the directions they have taken with their research. One ending can be the beginning to other great ideas. Just make sure to celebrate all of the learning and professional accomplishments along the way.

WHY THIS MODEL?

The authors want to thank Gail Ritchie for sharing this chapter on the Fairfax County Public Schools Teacher Researcher Network with us for this book. As we were researching various types of learning communities around the world, this group stood out to us as a well-organized, far-reaching entity from which others could learn a great deal. If you are just beginning a community of learners, this model is probably a bit overwhelming for you to think about setting up. However, we hope it offers bits of information from which you can draw to fit your group's needs. And, we hope it provides a big picture of the possibilities out there. Next, we close with our Epilogue.

Epilogue: Supporting and Sustaining Professional Collaboration

How to Use This Chapter

Congratulations on reading and learning about teacher research collaboratives.

The purpose of this Epilogue is to look at the future of teacher research learning communities and how they act as a valuable tool for developing professionalism in teaching. The future of collaborative teacher research rests on those teachers and researchers who value professional development and continue to use it as a tool to empower teachers to make appropriate instructional decisions for their students. Communities need to provide opportunities where teachers can freely choose the type of research they wish to explore. Imposing research topics on collaborative communities can discourage teachers from using action research as a means to develop professionally.

A useful way to promote teacher collaboratives in the future is to encourage teachers to start book clubs where they can engage in reading and discussing book selections on topics of common educational interest. There are many social networks that have organized book clubs and it seems to make sense that teachers also have professional book clubs as a means to collaborate and socialize. This would allow teachers to take part in a collaborative process without having to organize around a formal research agenda that may or may not have a direct impact on student achievement.

Finally, one of the key messages in this book and one that should guide future collaborative groups is that special expertise and knowledge of teachers be recognized and valued. Teachers should be supported in their efforts to develop and share their expertise by allowing them to conduct action research in a way that fosters professional learning.

FUTURE DIRECTIONS COLLABORATIVE GROUPS CAN CONSIDER

The following suggestions are based on materials contributed by the feedback we conducted and can be used as starting points for discussion when establishing or evaluating your collaborative group.

Organizational Suggestions

Organization is a key component to success of a collaborative group. As issues are raised and decisions are made about the organizational structures, the group establishes practices and protocols that will guide its success as it proceeds. When groups conduct initial meetings, the following summary of key points may be used to guide the discussion:

- Help new members be successful by asking them to complete prior commitments before joining a collaborative group. This will allow them to focus more on the tasks of the group and not feel overwhelmed.
- Consider seeking grants to support the research and help purchase books or other supplies to help the group function effectively while in collaboration.
- Goal setting is very important to the success of collaborative groups. Goals should always be established with supporting rationales and a time line for accomplishments.
- Recruit teachers who teach students across the life span and increase gender, age, and racial or ethnic diversity in the group.
- To widen networks, find ways for larger numbers of people to form satellite groups in their individual schools and community groups.
- Forge connections with other progressive educational networks and institutions.

Behavioral Suggestions

Once organizational structures of the group have been established, it will be important to pay attention to behavior expectations of the members. Asking key questions about how the group will respond or act in specific situations is an important discussion to have. This will minimize problems in the future and allow the group to be more effective in accomplishing its goals. Following is a summary of key points the group can use when discussing the behavior expectations of group members:

- Collaborate with community groups related to the research.
- Designate group members to narrate events and become the source of information for others.
- Make a list of ten behavioral expectations of the group related to responsibilities and problem-solving strategies.

Motivational Suggestions

Motivation to be included in a collaborative group can be used as a tool to fuel inspiration and success. If a group member lacks motivation, he or she may no longer feel his or her voice or contribution matters. The following ideas may increase a collaborative group's motivation to complete the task:

- Pursue research to improve instruction and create curriculum.
- Plan an inquiry conference to share ideas.
- Do more real-classroom observations and develop questions through observations.
- Investigate publishing the research.
- Present at conferences and develop teacher workshops about study groups.

Technical Suggestions

Members of a collaborative group may have individual technical skills they can contribute. Understanding the strength of each member's technical skills and using those strengths to guide the goals of the collaborative group will allow the group to be collectively successful. The following key points will help you focus on individual and group technical skills with the goal of enhancing the group:

- Pilot ways to study or own the research more effectively.
- Start new master's programs that support teachers.
- Create more policy for professional development and research in the classroom that will support teachers.
- Create a Web site connected to the research.
- Go global to network with others throughout the world.
- Understand publishing and editing strengths of members to increase publication success.

The remaining part of this chapter will introduce you to additional resources that will help you when working in teacher research collaboratives. In addition, you will hear stories from other teacher researchers who offer perspectives on actions and advocacy for teacher research collaboratives. Before reading this chapter, think critically about the following questions and consider writing down your responses in order to reflect on them after reading this chapter.

COLLABORATIVE WAYS OF THINKING TO INCREASE SUCCESS

Suggestions to aid in a long-term and productive project follow:

- Keep an open door policy to discuss research with other group members.
- Support multiple perspectives or perceptual strategies for thinking and looking at things from another's perspective while withholding negative criticism and offering more positive connections.
- Obtain time from department chairs or school administrators to provide access to principals whenever necessary.
- Pursue research topics that are authentic and driven by teachers and not by others uninvolved with the study.
- Collect sample research on similar topics but evaluated with an understanding that it doesn't have to be done the same way.
- Develop strategies for being critical with research.
- Provide financial resources for classroom libraries.
- Secure time to meet at conferences like the National Reading Conference. Consider organizing research getaway trips.
- Secure an outside evaluator to support thinking and data collection or analysis processes.

ENCOURAGING LONGEVITY THROUGH PROFESSIONAL REFLECTION

Using reflection as an evaluation tool of collaborative group members will enhance the longevity of the group. Reflection is a healthy way to focus on accomplishments and areas of improvements. Use the following questions to guide reflection before or after groups meet:

1. What compelling resource can I use from this book to help establish teacher research collaboratives?

2. What fears do I need to overcome when working in collegial relationships with my peers?

3. Will working in a collaborative group allow me to utilize my strengths and talents in a way that supports the group's mission and goals?

4. How can my experiences promote positive actions and advocacy for novice teacher researchers who want to get involved in learning communities as a way to grow professionally and work collectively in today's classrooms?

Professional development resources help define collaborative group goals and aid in supplying information that activates relevant knowledge on research topics of interest. Professional development resources can also encourage ongoing discovery of new knowledge as well as spark content inquiry questions relevant to the research. Knowledge gained from reading professional development resources also aids in providing individuals and collaboratives with new perspectives from which to view existing research. Think about some of your favorite professional development resources, and share these with your group.

CONCLUSION

The goals of this book were to open your mind to the many possibilities of collaborative learning—and professional development. This book has offered you a model to build collaborative bridges between those who are doing this type of research and professional development and those who wish to begin building a collaborative research community. If you have gained insights into the following processes, then our goal for writing this book has been met.

• You understand how to use collaboration as professional development.

• You understand the different group dynamics of collaborative research groups and how the dynamics of the group help or hinder successful outcomes.

• You understand what collaborative strategies are successful and not-so-successful.

• You understand the types of teacher research collaboratives and the effective implementation processes.

• You understand how to use technology as an online collaborative networking tool that produces effective results.

Whether you are already engaged in a collaborative research community or are planning to start one, our goal with this book is to provide you with tools and resources that will enable your community to succeed. We wish you luck in your collaborative group endeavors and invite you to use this book as a resource tool to fuel discussion and increase the success of your group. We would love to hear your collaborative group success stories or even pitfalls. Tell us what you have learned or changed. Do not be afraid to consider new ways of collaboration as we educators approach a new era of responsibility. E-mail us:

Cindy Lassonde: Lassonc@oneonta.edu

Susan Israel: SueIsrael@comcast.net

APPENDIX

Tools and Templates

You are welcome to reproduce and use the forms in this Appendix to fit the needs of your group. These forms are a collection of what others have found to be helpful in the collaborative process. Forms 1 through 6 are referenced in Chapter Four, and Forms 7 through 11 are referenced in Chapter Five.

Form 1

Stage 1: Getting to Know Invited Members

Who Should Be Invited to Be Part of the Group?

1. Who can offer a certain expertise or a unique perspective to the group?
    _____
    _____

2. Who would have the time and ability to commit to such a project?
    _____
    _____

3. Who might act as an outside consultant or short-term advisor to the group?
    _____
    _____

4. Data Collection
    _____
    _____

    a. What data will help answer the research questions?
        _____
        _____

    b. Who can help collect this data?
        _____
        _____

5. How many members should be invited to join the group?
    _____
    _____

What Are Key "First Discussions" to Have?

1. What do we hope to achieve from this collaboration?
    _____
    _____

2. What is our mission?

   _____

   _____

   a. What is the purpose of our group? How will students benefit?

      _____

      _____

   b. What are we doing to address this purpose?

      _____

      _____

   c. What philosophy or beliefs guide our work?

      _____

      _____

3. How will we communicate?

   _____

   _____

4. Meeting Logistics and Anticipated Timetable

   _____

   _____

   a. How often will we meet?

      _____

      _____

   b. Where?

      _____

      _____

   c. How long? (hours)

      _____

      _____

   d. How long do we anticipate the study will take? (number of weeks or months)

      _____

      _____

5. How will we support each other throughout the process?

   _____

   _____

6. What will we do if someone has to drop out of the group?

   _____

   _____

Form 2

Stage 1: Brainstorming Chart: Whom to Invite to the Group

The Teacher Research Process	Whom to Invite	How Collaborators Might Contribute
1. Identify the inquiry		
2. Develop purposes and potential research questions for the study		
3. Research the topic for a theoretical framework		

4. Design and organize a research plan		
5. Collect, organize, and analyze data		
6. Determine the results of the study		
7. Share the conclusions and implications		

Form 3

Stage 2: Sharing Perspectives and Talents

What perspectives do group members offer?

_____
_____
_____
_____
_____
_____
_____
_____
_____

What procedures will the group follow?

_____
_____
_____
_____
_____
_____
_____
_____
_____

What roles will group members play?

_____
_____
_____
_____
_____
_____
_____
_____
_____

Form 4

Tentative Agenda for Meetings

To: _____

_____ (list all members)

Tentative agenda for _____ (date) meeting

Place: _____

Time: _____

Please review the following agenda. If you want to add anything or make any revisions to it, please let me know by _____ (date prior to the meeting) by _____ (how you want them to respond). Thank you.

(your name and preferred contact information) _____

_____

Review and Approval of Minutes

Quick Group Evaluation

Old Business

    Follow-up items:

_____

_____

    Reports of actions taken since last meeting:

_____

_____

New Business

    High-priority items:

_____

_____

    Quick questions:

_____

_____

    Important items:

_____

_____

    Low-priority items:

_____

_____

Actions to Take/Person Responsible: _____

Scheduling of Next Meeting: _____

Form 5

Meeting Minutes

Date of Meeting: _____

Meeting Began: _____ (time) and Ended: _____ (time)

Members Present:

_____

_____

_____

_____

Members Absent:

_____

_____

_____

_____

These Items Were Discussed	Action to Be Taken and by Whom

Next Meeting Will Be: _____ (date) at _____ (time)

in _____ (where)

Form 6

Roles Signup Sheet

Role	Duties	Responsible Member(s)
Group Leader	Convene group; overall voice and contact person for group	
Group Recordkeeper	Organize and maintain data files	
Group Recorder	Agenda and minutes	
Group Research Checker(s)	Scope out scientifically based research on a topic as needed	
Group Teacher Research Expert(s)	Resource for how to go about doing teacher research	
Group Conflict Resolver(s)	Act as mediators	
Group Evaluator(s)	Ongoing evaluation; report to group	
Other Experts:		

Form 7

Stage 3: Supporting Each Other's Efforts and Learning

How can collaborative teacher research group members support each other in the steps of the process?

How will members support each other's ideas?

Form 8

Stage 4: Exploring the Possibilities

How will the group evaluate its progress along the way?

What will become of our results and findings?

What final reflections would the group share?

Form 9

Ongoing Group Evaluation

GROUP DYNAMICS

Do members actively engage in discussions and make meaningful contributions?

☐ Always ☐ Mostly ☐ Sometimes ☐ Infrequently ☐ Never

Do they come to the group prepared to participate?

☐ Always ☐ Mostly ☐ Sometimes ☐ Infrequently ☐ Never

Do members sincerely listen to and build off of each other's ideas?

☐ Always ☐ Mostly ☐ Sometimes ☐ Infrequently ☐ Never

Do members encourage and support the ideas of others?

☐ Always ☐ Mostly ☐ Sometimes ☐ Infrequently ☐ Never

Do members seek out and contribute resources to the group?

☐ Always ☐ Mostly ☐ Sometimes ☐ Infrequently ☐ Never

TEACHER RESEARCH COMPONENTS

At all times is there an air of inquisitiveness and questioning?

☐ Always ☐ Mostly ☐ Sometimes ☐ Infrequently ☐ Never

Is the research plan and design thoroughly thought out and are all members knowledgeable about the process?

☐ Always ☐ Mostly ☐ Sometimes ☐ Infrequently ☐ Never

Do members treat subjects and colleagues fairly, with confidentiality, honestly, and with mindful sensitivity to their needs?

☐ Always ☐ Mostly ☐ Sometimes ☐ Infrequently ☐ Never

Is all data clearly labeled, organized, accessible to members, and securely stored?

☐ Always ☐ Mostly ☐ Sometimes ☐ Infrequently ☐ Never

Are resources and ideas critically evaluated and discussed with members?

☐ Always ☐ Mostly ☐ Sometimes ☐ Infrequently ☐ Never

Are multiple perspectives considered, sorted, and brought together when appropriate through discussion?

☐ Always ☐ Mostly ☐ Sometimes ☐ Infrequently ☐ Never

But at the same time, is there room for divergent, creative thinking?

☐ Always ☐ Mostly ☐ Sometimes ☐ Infrequently ☐ Never

Are applications to and implications for students' learning always in the forefront of the study?

☐ Always ☐ Mostly ☐ Sometimes ☐ Infrequently ☐ Never

Form 10

Final Reflections

Discuss the following questions with your group:

1. What have we accomplished in our collaboration? How does this relate to our mission statement?

2. What group behaviors, procedures, and contributions were productive? How could we improve them?

3. What group behaviors, procedures, and contributions were unproductive? How would we change them the next time?

4. Will the group work together again? In what capacity? What will it study?

Form 11

Stage 5: Ongoing Conversations

What can I continue to offer my colleagues so we can develop deeper understandings of how our study's findings apply to students?

How can I continue to learn from the expertise of my colleagues?

APPENDIX

Reflection Questions

PART ONE: WHY SUPPORT COLLABORATIVE RESEARCH?

Chapter One: Improving Teacher Professional Learning

1. What are your views of teacher research? How do you define it?
2. What are your goals for participating in collaborative teacher research?
3. In which types of professional development have you participated? Which have you found most and least effective over time? To what do you attribute this?
4. What do you see as valuable components of Jane Hansen's description of how her collaborative learning community works together in this chapter's Thinking Together feature? How will you incorporate these ideas into the work of your collaborative group?

Chapter Two: Initiating Educational Improvements

1. What are the similarities and differences among the models of collaboration presented in this chapter?
2. What additional positive outcomes do you see demonstrated by these models?
3. How do each of these models empower teachers and students?

PART TWO: BUILDING A PROFESSIONAL LEARNING COMMUNITY

Chapter Three: Understanding the Inquiry Process

1. Have you ever experienced the phenomenon of the Invisible Researcher as described in the Effective Implementation feature of this chapter? What could be its advantages and disadvantages?
2. What do you know about teacher research? What is the group's collective knowledge and consensus about the steps?
3. How is the Readers' Theater script included in this chapter an example of collaboration? How might it build collaborative relationships among colleagues?

Chapter Four: Getting Started

1. How do each of the stages presented in this chapter apply to your group and its intended purpose and goals? How do you see your group evolving as you work together? What do you see as the unique strengths that individuals bring to your group? What might affect the ebb and flow of members' participation over time?

2. We often hear people say that if you bring food to a meeting, people will come. Lenski mentions coffee in her contribution to this chapter. What effect do you think food and drinks have on a meeting?

3. What role or roles do you see yourself best suited for in a collaborative group? Why?

4. Based on your answers to the questions raised by Christine Mallozzi in the final pages of this chapter, is collaboration right for you at this time? If not, what would make it right for you?

Chapter Five: Staying Productive

1. How does each stage presented in this chapter apply to your group and its intended purpose and goals?

2. What dilemmas do you foresee might occur in your group? How might your group avoid them? What problem-solving tactics would you employ if such dilemmas do occur?

3. If you were to create a rubric to evaluate your group's work together, what components would be included? How would you define success and failure in a group?

PART THREE: COLLABORATING EFFECTIVELY

Chapter Six: Ethical Considerations: Improving Group Dynamics

1. How do you define terms such as *ethics*, *values*, *right*, and *wrong*? How does your professional organization define them? Do all of your perceptions mesh, or are there some conflicts?

2. After reading this chapter, return to the questions posed on the chapter's first page and reflect on how you would respond to them.

3. How would you respond to the ethical situations posed throughout the chapter?

Chapter Seven: Leadership Strategies for Collaborative Support Groups

1. How do the strategies discussed in this chapter apply to your group and its intended purpose and goals?

2. Can your group identify effective leadership strategies that make your collaborative operate in a productive and positive manner? Does everyone in your group follow the same strategies?

3. Have you identified individual members' strengths so as to maximize their time and minimize some frustrations?

4. What challenges does your collaborative group face when planning meetings or sharing research projects?

5. How can your group focus on increasing effective strategies and reducing ineffective ones that cause problems for the progress and collegiality of group members?

6. What problems do you think your group might face and what strategies will you establish to overcome these problems?

7. What strategies do you see changing as your group engages in the various stages of a collaborative research project?

8. What kind of strategies as a leader will you establish as new members become involved with your project?

PART FOUR: MODEL LEARNING COMMUNITIES IN ACTION

Chapter Eight: School-Based and Partnership Communities

1. How do you see school-university partnerships and lesson study research fitting into your study or your group? What applications, benefits, and conflicts do you foresee? How might you avoid the conflicts?

2. What problems might lie ahead as the partners in the Collaborations at Work Feature 1—SUNY College at Oneonta and Mt. Markham Central School—proceed with their collaboration? How might these problems be unraveled?

Chapter Nine: Networking and Online Collaborations

1. How can technology be used with online collaboratives in an ethical manner within your research community?

2. What online collaborative resources are available that can help with communication, such as Microsoft products or Blackboard or Angel discussion boards?

3. What roles will be established when setting up an online collaborative and what are the responsibilities of the group members?

4. Will the online collaborative consider meeting at annual conferences?

Chapter Ten: A Districtwide Model: The Fairfax County Public Schools Teacher Research Network

1. What are the strengths of the Network's organization? What factors contribute to its success? What improvements might you suggest?

2. How is accountability woven into the fabric of the Network?

3. Often teachers avoid getting involved in learning communities because they do not feel they have the time or energy to commit to them. In light of this, why do you think this Network is so successful and widespread?

Epilogue: Supporting and Sustaining Professional Collaboration

1. How does each strategy discussed in this chapter apply to your group and its intended purpose and goals?

2. What else should your group consider before beginning teacher research in a collaborative group?

3. Are there inhibitions on the part of group members that need to be discussed?

4. How will your teacher research collaborative begin to take action and become an advocate for teacher research groups?

5. What problems do you think your group might face and what strategies will you establish to overcome these problems?

6. What ethical dilemmas do you foresee might occur in your group? How might your group avoid them? What problem-solving tactics would you employ if such ethical dilemmas do occur?

APPENDIX

Study Group Exercises

THROUGHOUT THE BOOK

The following exercises suggest ways to expand your thinking as you work through all chapters of this book:

1. Begin a response journal in which you write comments, questions, and notes as you read each chapter. When you come to discuss your readings with the group, use members' responses to prompt conversations and clarify understandings.
2. Read the Reflection Questions in Appendix B, and think about your responses before attending the group meeting. Make notes in your journal about these questions.

PART ONE: WHY SUPPORT COLLABORATIVE RESEARCH?

1. Make two columns regarding your participation in collaborative teacher research. Title one column "Things I'm Looking Forward to." Name the other column "Concerns I Have." Brainstorm your lists of responses in each column. Add to this list as you move through the book. When your group meets to discuss the chapters, share your lists. Note and discuss recurring themes that group members had. Discuss ways to promote success and longevity in your group based on what you have learned from this chapter. Make note of these preventative and problem-solving strategies in your journal for future reference.
2. Preview Form 1 in Appendix A to begin to reflect upon setting up your group.

PART TWO: BUILDING A PROFESSIONAL LEARNING COMMUNITY

Once you have discussed some strategies that make collaborative groups effective, reflect on the individual strengths as a collaborative group member that you can offer. What weaknesses do you have that might prevent you from functioning effectively within a group?

PART THREE: COLLABORATING EFFECTIVELY

After reading Chapter Seven, respond to the following statements in your response journal. Discuss them with your group to establish collaborative guidelines.

Recall a time when you were involved with a collaborative group with a leader who was effective and identify strategies that made this group effective. What were the elements of the group's overall effectiveness? When your collaborative group reviews the list of effective leadership strategies, discuss the strategies recalled that will be effective or ineffective ones for your group. Predict any challenges you think your group might face.

While reading this chapter, identify key strategies that you think will work with your group to help your research project be successful.

PART FOUR: MODEL LEARNING COMMUNITIES IN ACTION

1. Sketch the following t-chart into your response journal. Then, as you read the chapters in this part of the book, use the columns of the chart to organize your thoughts as you note the benefits and concerns or conflicts that the types of collaborative teacher research groups discussed in these chapters might present to your study or to the personality of your group.

Types of Collaborations	Benefits	Concerns or Conflicts
School-based groups		
School-university partnerships		
Networking groups		
Lesson-study groups		

2. As you read Chapter Ten, write comments, questions, and notes in your response journal. Refer to your journal entries during discussions with your group about the hows, whos, whats, and whys of setting up and running a teacher researcher network. You may think your group is not ready to tackle such a complex project as this in its entirety. However, as you read each section, reflect on what components and suggestions apply to your group and its goals. Allow this chapter to stretch your thinking to include and consider possibilities you hadn't even thought existed.

APPENDIX

Valuable Resources

Teachers Taking Action: A Comprehensive Guide to Teacher Research, by Lassonde and Israel, and *The Collaborative Teacher Research Handbook: A Guide to Establishing Effective Learning Communities*, which serves as a helpful companion book to *Teachers Taking Action*. Edited by the same authors, *The Collaborative Teacher Research Handbook* provides how-to guidelines for the processes of initiating, managing, completing, and sharing teacher research studies. Learn the steps of doing teacher research in *Teachers Taking Action*, then learn to form and maintain a collaborative group of researchers in *The Collaborative Teacher Research Handbook*.

"Critical Issue: Finding Time for Professional Development" from the North Central Regional Educational Laboratory. This site offers video clips from experts on professional development, such as Linda Darling-Hammond, and information on effective components of professional development initiatives. Available from www.ncrel.org/sdrs/areas/issues/educatrs/profdevl/pd300.htm.

You can set up an electronic group to communicate with members between meetings by creating an e-group account at www.groups.yahoo.com/local/news.html. Or, you could create an online blog at http://home.services.spaces.live.com/. You may also use the postings as part of the data in your research. More information about online collaboration software and methods is available in Chapter Nine of this book.

We have found Beebe and Masterson's long-respected book (2005) on group development, currently in its eighth edition, very helpful in working with groups. The group psychology information presented applies easily to teacher research situations. Also, Garmston and Wellman's book *The Adaptive School: A Sourcebook for Developing Collaborative Groups* (2008) on developing collaborative groups is a helpful sourcebook. Finally, if you are interested in reading further about methods teachers have used to work through ethical situations in teaching and teacher research, you will want to read *The Ethical Educator: Integrating Ethics Within the Context of Teaching and Teacher Research* (Israel & Lassonde, 2007). See the References section for these citations along with other informative texts on group psychology and behaviors.

Effective leaders can also gain further knowledge about leadership strategies through the Teachers Network Leadership Institute at www.teachersnetwork.org, which was created to improve students' learning by bringing teachers' voices to educational policymaking through the dissemination of action research findings.

Visit the Lesson Study Research Group homepage from Teachers College, Columbia University. It provides information, networking opportunities, and resources about lesson study. Available at www.tc.edu/lessonstudy/lessonstudy.html.

Diane Painter is the director of an international discussion board. This online network was established to assist teacher researchers. Those interested should contact Diane Painter at painter@hood.edu to learn more about how to obtain a name and password login.

The International Conference for Teacher Research is a wonderful way to meet other teacher researchers who are engaging in similar research projects. The conference usually runs following the annual conference of the American Educational Research Association (same city, same week). Go to www.bankstreet.edu/gs/teacherresearch.html for more information.

APPENDIX

Teacher Research Survey

Because much of the research and the voices of many quoted in this book resulted from survey responses, we have included the survey questions here for your reference. Reading through the questions and responding to them yourself may help you reflect on your own collaboration, or it may help you consider possibilities for collaboration about which you hadn't thought. Here is the survey.

Teacher Research Survey

Name: _____ Affiliation: _____

E-mail: _____ Phone: _____

Brief description of your background (years of teaching, positions you've held, grades taught, and so on):

Name of your collaborative teacher research group:

FOUNDING THE GROUP

1. Please describe how and why your group decided to work together.

---

2. What procedures were particularly helpful to you as you were learning about and setting up your group?

Organizing the Group

3. Who are the members of your group?

What are their positions, institutions, and roles in your research group?

4. How is your group organized?

Meeting frequency and times:

Mission statement:

Paperwork:

Integration of technology:

The Focus for the Group

5. What is the theme of your group?

6. How did your group go about deciding its theme or what it will research?

What were the thought processes here?

What strategies did you use to identify areas of literacy that needed attention?

STRENGTHS AND CHALLENGES

7. What are the strengths of your group?

8. What are the stumbling blocks you have come up against or anticipate having?

9. Share how you have attempted to avoid or overcome stumbling blocks.

What has worked?

What hasn't?

METHODOLOGICAL CONSIDERATIONS

10. What resources and tools have you found helpful in your collaborative work?

Why?

Please e-mail us any sample forms that you have found to have been particularly helpful in your collaboration. Note on the forms who created them so we can give credit.

11. What resources have you wished you had?

IMPACT OF THE **G**ROUP

12. What evidence do you have that your group's work has influenced teaching and learning in the classroom?

13. What evidence do you have that your group's work has influenced teaching at the local, regional, and/or national level also?

FUTURE **D**IRECTIONS

14. How do you see your group developing from here?

15. What are your future goals?

OTHER

16. Is there anything else you'd like to say about your group?

17. What questions would you liked answered about working in collaborative teacher research groups?

References

Appley, E. G., & Winder, A. E. (1977). An evolving definition of collaboration and some implications for the world of work. *The Journal of Applied Behavioral Science, 13*(3), 279–291.

ARDDP. (2008). Partnerships for improving literacy in urban schools: Advanced reading development demonstration project. *The Reading Teacher, 61*(8).

Arter, J. (2001, Spring). Learning teams: The way to go for professional development. *Classroom Assessment Connections.* Portland, OR: Assessment Training Institute, Inc.

Au, K. H. (2005). *Multicultural issues and literacy achievement.* New York: Taylor and Francis.

Au, K. H., Raphael, T. E., & Mooney, K. (In press a). Improving reading achievement in elementary schools: Guiding change in a time of standards. In S. B. Wepner & D. S. Strickland (Eds.), *Supervison of reading programs* (4th ed.). New York: Teachers College Press.

Au, K. H., Raphael, T. E., & Mooney, K. (In press b). What we have learned about teacher education to improve literacy achievement in urban schools. In V. Chou, L. Morrow, & L. Wilkinson (Eds.), *Improving the preparation of teachers of reading in urban settings: Policy, practice, pedagogy.* Newark, DE: International Reading Association.

Avery, L. M. (2003). Knowledge, identity, and teachers' communities of practice. Unpublished doctoral dissertation, Cornell University, Ithaca, NY.

Avery, L. M., & Carlsen, W. S. (2001). Knowledge, identity, and teachers' multiple communities of practice. Paper presented at the annual meeting of the National Association for Research in Science Teaching, St. Louis, MO, March 25–28.

Bandura, A. (1986). *Social foundations of thought and action: A social cognitive theory.* Englewood Cliffs, NJ: Prentice Hall.

Baumfield, V., & Butterworth, M. (2007). Creating and translating knowledge about teaching and learning in collaborative school–university research partnerships: an analysis of what is exchanged across the partnerships, by whom and how. *Teachers and Teaching, 13*(4), 411–427.

Beebe, S. A., & Masterson, J. (2000). *Communicating in small groups: Principles and practices* (6th ed.). New York: Longman.

Beebe, S. A., & Masterson, J. (2005). *Communicating in small groups: Principles and practices* (8th ed.). New York: Allyn & Bacon.

Bullough, R. V., Jr., & Gitlin, A. D. (2001). *Becoming a student of teaching: Linking knowledge production and practice* (2nd ed.). New York: Routledge/Falmer.

Bullough, R. V., Jr., & Pinnegar, S. (2001). Guidelines for quality in autobiographical forms of self-study research. *Educational Researcher, 30*(3), 13–21.

Burant, T. J., Gray, C., Ndaw, E., McKinney-Keys, V., & Allen, G. (2007). Part I: Advancing the conversation: The rhythms of a teacher research group. *Multicultural Perspectives, 9*(1), 10–18.

Cisar, S. H. (2005). Collaborative teacher research: Learning with students. *Foreign Language Annals, 38*(1), 77–89.

Cochran-Smith, M., & Lytle, S. L. (1993). *Inside/outside: Teacher research and knowledge.* New York: Teachers College Press.

Cochran-Smith, M., & Lytle, S. L. (1999). The teacher research movement: A decade later. *Educational Researcher, 28*(7), 15–25.

Covey, S. R. (2004). *The 7 habits of highly effective people: Powerful lessons in personal change.* New York: The Free Press.

Cuban, L. (1992). Curriculum stability and change. In P. Jackson, *Handbook of Research on Curriculum.* New York, Macmillan, 216–248.

Cunningham, C. M. (2005). *The effect of teachers' sociological understanding of science on classroom practice and curriculum innovation.* Ithaca, NY: Cornell University.

Dobbs, K. (2000, January). Simple moments of learning. *Training Magazine, 37*(1), 52.

Fairfax County Public Schools (FCPS). (2007). *Student achievement goals.* Retrieved on June 1, 2007 from www.fcps .edu/schlbd/sg/goals.htm.

Falk-Ross, F., & Cuevas, P. (2008). Getting the big picture: An overview of the teacher research process. In Lassonde, C. A., & Israel, S. E. (Eds.). *Teachers taking action: A comprehensive guide to teacher research.* Newark, DE: International Reading Association.

Forsyth, D. R. (2005). *Group dynamics.* New York: Wadsworth.

Fuhrer, U. (2004). *Cultivating minds: Identity as meaning-making practice.* New York: Taylor and Francis.

Garmston, R. J., & Wellman, B. M. (1999). Better by the bunch. *Journal of Staff Development, 20*(4), 64–65.

Garmston, R. J., & Wellman, B. M. (2008). *The adaptive school: A sourcebook for developing collaborative groups.* Norwood, MA: Christopher-Gordon.

Goatley, V., Highfield, K., Bentley, J., Pardo, L. S., Folkert, J., Scherer, P., Raphael, T. E., & Grattan, K. (1994). Empowering teachers to be researchers: A collaborative approach. *Teacher Research: The Journal of Classroom Inquiry, 1*(2), 128–144.

Gold, N., & Powe, K. W. (2001). *Assessing the impact and effectiveness of professional development in the advanced technological education (ATE) program.* Kalamazoo, MI: The Evaluation Center of Western Michigan University.

Goldman, S. R. (2005). Designing for scalable educational improvement: Process of inquiry in practice. In C. Dede, J. P. Honan, & L. C. Peters (Eds.), *Scaling up success: Lessons learned from technology-based educational improvement* (pp. 67–96). San Francisco: Jossey-Bass.

Gullickson, A., Lawrenz, F., & Keiser, N. (2000). *Assessing the impact and effectiveness of the Advanced Technological Education (ATE) program: Status report 2.* Kalamazoo, MI: The Evaluation Center, Western Michigan University.

Henson, R. K. (2001). The effect of participation in teacher research professional development on teacher efficacy and empowerment. Paper presented at the Annual Meeting of the Mid-South Educational Research Association. (Little Rock, AR, November 13–16, 2001).

Israel, S. E., & Lassonde, C. A. (2007). *The ethical educator: Integrating ethics within the context of teaching and teacher research.* New York: Peter Lang.

Jacob, E. (2000). Integrating technology and pedagogy in a cultural foundations course. *Journal of Computing in Teacher Education, 16*(4), 12–17.

Johnson, M. A., & Johnson, G. A. (1999). The insiders: Development in school with colleagues can succeed. *Journal of Staff Development, 20*(4), 27–29.

Johnston, M., & Kerper, R. M. (1996). Positioning ourselves: Parity and power in collaborative work. *Curriculum Inquiry, 26*(1), 5–24.

Katzenbach, J. R., & Smith, D. K. (2003). *The wisdom of teams: Creating the high-performance organization.* New York: HarperCollins.

Knight, S. L., Wiseman, D. L., & Cooner, D. (2000). Using collaborative teacher research to determine the impact of professional development school activities on elementary students' math and writing outcomes. *Journal of Teacher Education, 51*(1), 26–38.

Konopka, G. (1981). Perspectives on social group work. In S. Abels & P. Abels (Eds.), *Social Work with Groups: Proceedings 1979 Symposium* (pp. 111–116). Louisville, KY: Committee for the Advancement of Social Work with Groups.

Kowert, P. A. (2002). *Groupthink or deadlock: What do leaders learn from their advisors?* Albany, NY: State University of New York Press.

Lamon, M., Secules, T., Petrosino, A., Hackett, R., Bransford, J., & Goldman, S. (1996). Schools for thought: Overview of the project and lessons learned from one of the sites. In L. Schauble & R. Glaser (Eds.), *Innovations in Learning: New Environments for Education* (pp. 243–288). Mahwah, NJ: Erlbaum.

Lassonde, C., & Israel, S. (2008). *Teachers taking action: A comprehensive guide to teacher research.* Newark, DE: International Reading Association.

Lassonde, C., Stearns, K., & Dengler, K. (2005). What are you reading in book groups?: Developing reading lives in teacher candidates. *Action in Teacher Education, 27*(2), 43–53.

Lewin, K. (1948). *Resolving social conflicts: Selected papers on group dynamics.* New York: Harper & Row.

Lewis, C. (2002). *Lesson study: A handbook of teacher-led instructional change*. Philadelphia, PA: Research for Better Schools.

Louie, B. Y., Drevdahl, D. J., Purdy, J. M., & Stackman, R. W. (2003). Advancing the scholarship of teaching through collaborative self-study. *The Journal of Higher Education, 74*(2), 150–171.

MacLean, M. S., & Mohr, M. M. (1999). *Teacher-researchers at work*. Berkeley, CA: The National Writing Project.

McKenzie, J. (1991, April). Designing staff development for the information age. *The Educational Technology Journal 1*(4).

McLaughlin, M. W., & Talbert, J. (1993). *Contexts that matter for teaching and learning: Strategic opportunities for meeting the nation's educational goals*. Stanford, CA: Center for Research on the Context of Secondary School Teaching, Stanford University.

Meyer, J. W., & Rowan, B. (1975). *Notes on the structure of educational organizations*. San Francisco: American Sociological Association.

Meyer, J. W., & Rowan, B. (1977). Institutionalized organizations: Formal structure as myth and ceremony. *American Journal of Sociology, 83*(2), 340–363.

Mohr, M. M., Rogers, C., Sanford, B., Nocerino, M. A., MacLean, M. S., & Clawson, S. (2004). *Teacher research for better schools*. New York: Teachers College Press.

Morse, J. M. (1994). Designing funded qualitative research. In N. K. Denzin & Y. S. Lincoln (Eds.), *Handbook of qualitative research* (pp. 220–235). Thousand Oaks, CA: Sage.

National Staff Development Council (NSDC). (2007). *NSDC's standards for staff development*. Retrieved on June 2, 2007 from www.nsdc.org/standards/index.cfm.

Papert, S. (1994). *Children's machine: Rethinking school in the age of the computer*. New York: Perseus.

Radtke, J. M. (1998). *How to write a mission statement*. Retrieved August 1, 2007, from www.tgci.com/magazine/How%20to%20Write%20a%20Mission%20Statement.pdf.

Raphael, T. E., Florio-Ruane, S., & George, M. (2001). Book club plus: A conceptual framework to organize literacy instruction. *Language Arts, 79*(1), 159–168.

Raphael, T. E., Florio-Ruane, S., Kehus, M., George, M., Hasty, N. L., & Highfield, K. (2001). Thinking for ourselves: Literacy learning in a diverse teacher inquiry network. *The Reading Teacher, 54*(6), 596–607.

Richards, M., Elliott, A., Woloshyn, V., & Mitchell, C. (2001). *Collaboration uncovered: The forgotten, the assumed, and the unexamined in collaborative education*. New York: Bergin and Garvey.

Richardson, V. (1994). Conducting research on practice. *Educational Researcher, 23*, 5–10.

Ritchie, G. (2006). *Teacher research as a habit of mind*. (Doctoral dissertation. George Mason University, Fairfax, VA, 2006). *Digital Dissertations, AAT 3206130*.

Ross, M. R., Powell, S. R., & Elias, M. J. (2002). New roles for school psychologists: Addressing the social and emotional learning needs of students. *School Psychology Review, 31*(1).

Schoenfeld, A. H. (1999). The core, the canon and the development of research skills. In E. C. Legemann & L. S. Shulman (Eds.), *Issues in education research* (pp. 166–202). San Francisco: Jossey-Bass.

Scholtes, P. R., Joiner, B. L., & Streibel, B. J. (2003). *The team handbook* (3rd ed.). Salem, NH: GOAL/QPC and Oriel.

Secules, T., Cottom, C., Bray, M., & Miller, L. (1997). Creating schools for thought. *How Children Learn, 54*(6), 56–60.

Sipple, J. W. (1997). Toward an improved understanding of interest groups: A case study of business involvement in public education reform using political and institutional theories. *Education, The University of Michigan*, 252.

Stager, G. S. (1995). Laptop schools lead the way in professional development. *Educational Leadership, 53*(2), 78–81.

Tchudi, S. (Ed.). (1997). *Alternatives to grading student writing*. Urbana, IL: NCTE.

Trautmann, N., & MaKinster, J. (2005). *Teacher/scientist partnerships as professional development: Understanding how collaboration can lead to inquiry*. Paper presented at the 2005 International Conference of the Association for the Education of Teachers of Science, Colorado Springs, CO, January 19–23.

Tuckman, B. W. (1965). Developmental sequence in small groups. *Psychological Bulletin, 63*, 384–399.

Tuckman, B. W., & Jensen, M.A.C. (1977). Stages of small group development revisited. *Group and Organizational Studies, 2*, 419–427.

U.S. Department of Education. (2001). *No child left behind*. Available online at http://www.ed.gov/policy/elsec/leg/esea02/107–110.pdf. Retrieved August 9, 2007.

Vascellero, J. E. (2007, August 29). *New social-networking sites let professionals rub virtual elbows.* Available online at www.careerjournal.com/jobhunting/networking/20070829-vascellaro.html. Retrieved December 8, 2007.

Vaughn, G., & Hogg, M. (2002). *Introduction to social psychology* (3rd ed.). Sydney: Prentice Hall.

Ware, D., Mallozzi, C. A., Edwards, E. C., & Baumann, J. F. (2008). Collaboration in teacher research: Complicated cooperation. In C. A. Lassonde & S. E. Israel (Eds.), *Teachers taking action: A comprehensive guide to teacher research.* Newark, DE: International Reading Association.

Weick, K. E. (1976). Educational organizations as loosely coupled systems. *Administrative Science Quarterly, 21,* 1–19.

Wenger, E. (1998). *Communities of practice: Learning, meaning, and identity.* Cambridge, UK: Cambridge University Press.

Zeichner, K. (2003). Teacher research as professional development for P–12 educators in the USA. *Educational Action Research, 11,* 301–326.

Index